Generis

PUBLISHIN

TRADITIONAL CHINESE CULTURE LESSON PLAN WITH COOPERATING LEARNING METHOD (TCC& CLM)

WENWEN MA
Assistant Professor Dr. SAEID MOTEVALLI
Professor Dr. ROGAYAH BINTI A RAZAK

Title: **TRADITIONAL CHINESE CULTURE LESSON PLAN WITH COOPERATING LEARNING METHOD (TCC& CLM)**

ISBN: 979-8-89248-680-4

Author: WENWEN MA, Assistant Professor Dr. SAEID MOTEVALLI,Professor Dr. ROGAYAH BINTI A RAZAK

Cover image: www.unsplash.com

Publisher: Generis Publishing
Online orders: www.generis-publishing.com
Contact email: info@generis-publishing.com

TRADITIONAL CHINESE CULTURE LESSON PLAN WITH COOPERATING LEARNING METHOD (TCC& CLM)

Authors:

MA WENWEN

Assistant Professor Dr. SAEID MOTEVALLI

Professor Dr. ROGAYAH BINTI A RAZAK

2024

Acknowledgements

Writing a book is not a solitary endeavour, and we are immensely grateful for the invaluable support and assistance we have received from numerous individuals.

We extend our sincerest gratitude to the Faculty of Social Sciences and Liberal Arts (FOSSLA) at UCSI University, Kuala Lumpur, Malaysia. Their unwavering support and encouragement played a crucial role in making this book a reality. Without their assistance, this project may not have reached its completion, and we am truly thankful for their efforts.

To all those who offered their suggestions and help during the creation of this book, we are deeply appreciative of your contributions. Your insights and input have enriched this work and made it possible to share meaningful knowledge in the field of educational psychology and education.

Thank you all for being an integral part of this journey, and for your continued support in our pursuit of contributing to the realm of psychological research.

Preface

Chinese traditional culture is a complex and venerable aspect of human civilisation, intricately developed over millennia by the various ethnic groups residing in China. This lasting cultural heritage, encompassing diverse values, beliefs, rituals, and spiritual practices, including those articulated by Confucius and Laozi, is not only a remnant of history but a vibrant legacy that evokes national pride and increasing worldwide fascination. As educational institutions globally acknowledge the value of cultural understanding, the role of traditional Chinese culture in higher education has emerged as a matter of significant relevance and reflection.

This book explores the fundamental nature and impact of Chinese traditional culture as a foundational element of education in China, analysing its importance in cultivating moral values and improving educational quality. The inquiry starts with an overview of the profound origins and extensive influence of traditional Chinese cultural aspects. These characteristics have influenced, and persist in influencing, several aspects of Chinese society, including literature, the arts, medicine, and philosophy. Moreover, the book tackles the urgent need for educational reform to guarantee the preservation and successful integration of traditional culture within contemporary educational practices.

Instilling traditional culture education in Chinese higher education is essential for cultivating well-rounded individuals with both technical capabilities and a robust cultural identity. The book delineates that the fundamental concepts of harmony, balance, and moderation intrinsic to Chinese traditional culture promote moral growth and character building while providing students with essential insights to address modern social concerns. However, integrating these profound cultural values into the educational system presents several obstacles.

Modern educational institutions have several challenges in proficiently imparting traditional Chinese culture. A significant issue is the disconnection between conventional cultural education and students' daily experiences, resulting in diminished motivation and involvement among students. Furthermore, the book underscores the deficiencies in contemporary educational methodologies, which frequently prioritise rote memorisation over critical analysis and practical implementation. Furthermore, it addresses the limitations imposed by inadequately prepared educators and an educational setting that is poorly equipped to foster a profound respect for traditional culture.

This book argues for the reform of conventional cultural education to improve its relevance and accessibility in response to these problems. By amalgamating contemporary pedagogical methods with conventional curriculum and utilising collaborative learning frameworks, educators may cultivate a more participatory and engaging educational atmosphere. This methodology not only connects ancient knowledge with contemporary application but also fosters collaboration, enhances academic performance, and reinforces cultural identity among students.

Reform initiatives should prioritise the improvement of teacher training and development, guaranteeing that educators are adequately prepared to impart the nuances of traditional culture. The curriculum should be enhanced to provide experiential learning opportunities that align with the current circumstances of students, so expanding their educational experience and enhancing their cultural understanding.

This book aims to provide ideas and recommendations for revitalising traditional Chinese cultural education, emphasising its importance in fostering cultural identity, responsibility, and pride in a globalised society. This study seeks to rectify existing educational deficiencies and introduce creative reform tactics, therefore fostering a culturally cognisant and globally collaborative generation of students committed to preserving and disseminating the lasting legacy of Chinese civilisation.

Contents

CHAPTER ONE

INTRODUCTION

1.1 Introduction

Chapter explores the significance of Chinese traditional culture as a foundational element of Chinese civilization, developed over millennia by diverse ethnic groups. In higher education, this cultural education is crucial for shaping quality education and moral values and contributing to societal cultural growth. Nonetheless, educational institutions face significant challenges in effectively imparting traditional Chinese culture, necessitating reforms to enhance educational quality and effectiveness. The chapter emphasizes the transformative impact of Traditional Chinese Culture and Cooperative Learning Models (TCC & CLM) in cultivating cultural identity, boosting academic achievement, promoting teamwork, and benefiting educators and society. It also addresses current challenges, the limitations of traditional teaching methods, and the potential benefits of innovative cooperative learning approaches.

1.2.1 Importance of Chinese traditional culture

Chinese traditional culture, the cornerstone of Chinese civilization, has been shaped over thousands of years through the contributions of various ethnic groups. According to Wang (2021), it encompasses a complex web of values, beliefs, customs, and practices, including the cultural thoughts and spiritual concepts of Taoism and Confucianism as represented by the teachings of Laozi and Confucius. This culture integrates both material and non-material elements such as politics, economy, ideology, and art, and is characterized by a deep-rooted philosophical tradition that emphasizes harmony, balance, and moderation. These principles have profoundly influenced all aspects of Chinese culture, including literature, art, medicine, martial arts, science, technology, and daily life (Xie et al., 2021).

Moreover, Chinese traditional culture reflects the country's rich historical and cultural heritage, incorporating various religious and spiritual practices like Taoism, Buddhism, and folk religions. These practices have fostered a unique artistic and literary tradition, including classical Chinese poetry, calligraphy, painting, and music (Yu, 2019). In the realm of health and well-being, traditional practices such as Chinese medicine, acupuncture, and dietary therapy follow principles of equilibrium and harmony and have been passed down through generations.

As globalization progresses, the influence of Chinese traditional culture continues to expand, attracting increasing numbers of international learners to study the Chinese language and culture. Additionally, the concepts of harmony in Confucianism and environmental consciousness in Taoism offer valuable insights for addressing contemporary global issues and promoting international cooperation (Zhang, 2021). Thus, Chinese traditional culture holds significant historical and societal value and exerts a positive global impact. Understanding and preserving this culture not only fosters national pride and cultural confidence but also facilitates global cultural exchange and cooperation, contributing to a more harmonious world.

1.2.2 Importance of Chinese traditional culture education

Traditional Chinese culture education holds significant importance in Chinese higher education, serving as a core component of both quality education and moral education, as well as a key factor in societal cultural development. According to Xie

(2021), traditional culture education plays a crucial role in the moral development and character formation of contemporary college students, preparing them to become societal elites well-versed in both scientific knowledge and traditional culture.

Traditional culture education enhances students' moral cultivation and cultural identity. Systematic education in traditional culture allows students to gain a deeper understanding and appreciation of core Chinese cultural values, such as the Confucian ideals of harmony and the Daoist principles of naturalism. This understanding elevates their personal moral standards and provides valuable insights for addressing contemporary social issues (ibid).

Traditional culture education fosters a sense of social responsibility and historical mission in students. Scholars argue that it helps students better comprehend and carry forward the cultural heritage of the Chinese nation, boosting their cultural confidence and historical accountability (Jiang, 2019; Zhang, 2020). This cultural identity and responsibility inspire students to contribute positively to their future careers and societal roles.

Traditional culture education positively impacts students' academic achievement as well as learning motivation. Research by Luo and Liu (2019) indicates that students who receive traditional culture education exhibit higher levels of academic achievement and learning motivation. Engaging with traditional culture helps students find a cultural foundation within modern education, fostering a positive learning attitude and value system that better equips them to face future challenges.

In the context of globalization, traditional culture education holds substantial international influence. As China's status on the global stage continues to rise, the global influence of Chinese culture expands accordingly. Traditional culture education aids students in understanding and preserving their cultural heritage and promotes international cultural exchange and cooperation (Zhang, 2021).

Reinforcing traditional culture education in higher education is essential for the personal development of students and the broader goal of cultural preservation and innovation. Advancing traditional culture education in higher education is a vital pathway to enhancing educational quality and fostering well-rounded, culturally aware students.

1.2.3 Challenge of Chinese traditional culture education

The education of traditional Chinese culture in colleges and universities faces numerous challenges. Despite its recognized importance, several factors hinder its effective implementation.

Lack of motivation among college students to learn about traditional Chinese culture is among the most important issues that needs more attention. The decline of traditional culture in modern society and the influence of internet culture contribute to this disinterest (Zhang, 2024). Many students perceive traditional culture as outdated and irrelevant to their current lives and future careers.

Limited knowledge of traditional culture principles among students. Luo and Liu (2019) found that although 98.8% of students acknowledged the importance of traditional culture for China's development, only 39.5% felt they knew or understood some of the content. Most students lack knowledge about ancient Chinese thinkers, literary masterpieces, traditional festivals, and historical events. Insufficient emphasis on traditional culture education in the higher education curriculum contributes to this knowledge gap.

Unconducive learning environment for traditional culture education. Traditional culture in education typically focuses on activities like performances, calligraphy, and music, overlooking the deeper philosophical and ethical aspects (Li, 2016). Teaching methods often center on memorization and passive learning, lacking student engagement and critical thinking skill development. (Yan, 2020).

Inadequate qualifications of teachers could one of the most effective factors influencing the teaching and learning quality. Many teachers lack the necessary expertise in traditional Chinese culture and continue to use outdated teaching methods. This issue is more pronounced in science and engineering colleges, where traditional culture education is even more deficient compared to majors related to Chinese philosophy, history, and literature (Li, 2016).

Disconnection between Traditional Cultural Education and Students' Everyday Lives has been considered among fundamental topics of investigation. Research shows that traditional culture education in colleges has become separated from students' everyday experiences, with inadequate educational content, methods, and coverage (Ma et al., 2018). Chi and Xu (2018) highlighted that traditional culture education in private colleges suffers from lack of experiential learning and inadequate educational content, resulting in only 25% of students feeling that traditional culture education meets their learning needs.

Traditional Chinese culture education in higher education faces significant challenges. Lack of student motivation, limited knowledge of cultural principles, an unconducive learning environment, inadequately qualified teachers, and a disconnect from students' daily lives. Addressing these challenges is crucial for the effective integration and promotion of traditional culture education in colleges and universities.

1.2.4 Necessity of Reforming Traditional Chinese Culture Education

Reforming traditional Chinese culture education in colleges and universities is crucial to address numerous challenges and enhancing the overall quality and effectiveness of education.

One significant challenge is the disconnection between traditional culture education and students' daily lives, which necessitates reform. Traditional culture education has become increasingly detached from students' everyday experiences, with deficiencies in educational content, methods, and scope (Ma et al., 2018). To address this, curricula should integrate traditional culture with modern contexts, making it more relatable and meaningful for students. Furthermore, there is a need for innovative and interactive teaching methods to promote positive interactions between teachers and students, thereby enhancing the engagement and relevance of learning to students' lives." (Liu, 2019).

Among the topics that are being discussed, the lack of qualified teachers also presents a critical issue. Many educators lack the necessary expertise in traditional Chinese culture and continue to rely on outdated teaching methods (Yan, 2020). To overcome this, enhanced teacher training and development programs are essential, equipping educators with the knowledge and skills required to effectively teach traditional culture (Zhou et al., 2014).

Another challenge is the overemphasis on practical education at the expense of traditional culture education, which leads to a lack of knowledge and appreciation of traditional culture among college students. It is important to prioritize traditional culture education alongside practical education, ensuring that students receive a well-rounded education that includes both professional skills and cultural heritage (Zhang, 2024).

"By integrating traditional cultural education with modern technology, a more comprehensive and interactive learning environment can be established. Utilizing digital resources and online platforms can enhance the accessibility and engagement of traditional culture education (Chi & Xu, 2018).

Furthermore, traditional culture education should incorporate experiential learning activities that resonate with students' daily lives. This approach bridges the gap between traditional teachings and modern applications, making the learning experience more dynamic and impactful (Ma et al., 2018).

In conclusion, reforming traditional Chinese culture education is essential for preserving cultural heritage, enhancing educational quality, and fostering students' holistic development. Addressing these key issues will enable colleges and universities to create a more effective and engaging traditional culture education that meets the needs of contemporary students.

1.2 Significance of TCC& CLM

1.2.1 Cultivating Cultural Identity and Social Responsibility

Contemporary college students represent a vital force in societal development and progress. As they prepare to enter society and assume national responsibilities, establishing a correct worldview, outlook on life, and value system is crucial. Excellent traditional Chinese culture plays a significant role in achieving this goal (Su, 2022). Deeply rooted in Chinese history, traditional Chinese culture has shaped the values and beliefs of the Chinese people for thousands of years. Through learning and understanding traditional Chinese culture, contemporary college students can inherit and carry forward cultural heritage, cultivate cultural identity, and enhance social responsibility.

Traditional Chinese culture offers unique perspectives and methods to help contemporary college students address practical problems and promote social development. Confucian philosophy, for example, emphasizes the importance of social harmony and personal virtue. Through the study of Confucianism, college students learn how to establish harmonious relationships with others, cultivate moral character, and contribute to building a harmonious society (Fan, 2021). Traditional Chinese culture education in colleges is not only about cultural heritage but also an essential component of contemporary college students' education and development.

The advancement of globalization and cultural exchange makes cultivating students' cultural awareness and appreciation increasingly important. Traditional Chinese culture is a vital part of China's comprehensive national strength and reflects the core values and beliefs of the Chinese nation. Effective ideological guidance through traditional culture education is necessary for contemporary college students, enhancing their cultural identity and social responsibility and improving their competitiveness on the international stage.

Learning and understanding traditional Chinese culture are crucial for cultivating cultural identity and social responsibility among contemporary college students. Systematic traditional culture education allows students to deeply understand and identify with the core values of Chinese culture, enhancing cultural confidence and historical responsibility. This cultural identity and responsibility motivate students to contribute positively to their future careers and social lives.

1.2.2 Enhancing academic achievement and Learning Motivation

Traditional Chinese culture education has a demonstrably positive impact on students' academic achievement and learning motivation. Empirical evidence suggests that students exposed to traditional culture education exhibit superior academic achievement and higher levels of learning motivation (Luo and Liu, 2019). Engaging with traditional culture provides students with a foundational cultural context within modern education, fostering a positive learning attitude and a robust value system. Confucian philosophy, with its emphasis on social harmony and personal virtue, offers practical strategies for improving academic achievement. Through the study of Confucianism, students cultivate essential qualities such as discipline, respect, and diligence, which are critical for academic success (Fan, 2021). These attributes not only enhance academic achievement but also prepare students for future professional and personal challenges.

Traditional teaching methods often rely on rote memorization and passive learning, which fail to engage students effectively. In contrast, cooperative learning fosters active participation, critical thinking, and collaborative problem-solving, creating a more dynamic and engaging classroom environment. This approach helps students develop a deeper understanding of the material, thereby improving overall academic achievement. The cooperative learning method has proven particularly effective in enhancing students' learning motivation. Participation in cooperative learning activities encourages students to become more proactive learners and fosters a greater interest in Chinese traditional culture. This pedagogical approach promotes interactive and engaging exploration of subject matter, thereby increasing student motivation and enthusiasm for learning (Johnson & Johnson, 1994).

Integrating traditional Chinese culture education with cooperative learning methods significantly enhances students' academic achievement and learning motivation. This holistic educational model provides a more engaging and effective learning environment, thereby promoting both academic and personal growth. Through such an integrative approach, educators can better prepare students for success in the modern world.

1.2.3 Promoting Teamwork and Problem-Solving Skills

The cooperative learning method significantly enhances students' teamwork and problem-solving skills. Through collaboration with peers, students develop essential skills such as effective communication, active listening, and respect for diverse perspectives (Slavin, 2015). In a globalized society, these skills are crucial as individuals from various cultural and educational backgrounds must work together to solve complex problems.

Cooperative learning creates an environment where students communicate ideas, assign roles, and resolve conflicts. This cooperative approach improves teamwork abilities, interpersonal skills, and team cohesion. Students learn to rely on each other's strengths and support one another's learning, fostering a sense of community and mutual respect. Cooperative learning also significantly enhances students' problem-solving abilities. By tackling academic challenges together, students learn to view problems from multiple perspectives and develop creative solutions. This process cultivates critical thinking and analytical skills, essential for academic success and real-world problem-solving.

The application of cooperative learning in traditional Chinese culture education allows students to explore complex cultural and philosophical concepts in a collaborative setting. This method helps them gain a deeper understanding of the material and apply it to contemporary contexts. Integrating traditional cultural education with cooperative learning enables students to appreciate the relevance of cultural heritage in modern society and apply traditional principles to solve modern problems.

The teamwork and problem-solving skills developed through cooperative learning benefit students academically and prepare them for future professional environments. Employers highly value individuals who can collaborate effectively and solve problems. By fostering these skills in an educational setting, cooperative learning makes students more competitive and adaptable in their future careers.

Cooperative learning in traditional Chinese culture education significantly promotes teamwork and problem-solving skills. Through interactive and collaborative learning experiences, students acquire essential skills crucial for academic success and professional development. This holistic approach not only enhances students' understanding of traditional culture but also equips them with the competencies needed to navigate and succeed in a complex, interconnected world.

1.2.4 Benefits for Teachers, Schools, and Society

The application of cooperative learning methods in traditional Chinese culture education brings numerous benefits to teachers, schools, and society as a whole.

For teachers, cooperative learning offers an opportunity to move away from traditional teacher-centered approaches and explore innovative teaching strategies. Traditional methods emphasize rote memorization, limiting students' initiative and creativity. Cooperative learning creates a student-centered environment, encouraging students to actively explore knowledge and apply it to real-life situations. It promotes the development of teamwork and communication skills, essential for future professional success (Li et al., 2020).

Cooperative learning helps teachers integrate cultural elements more effectively into their teaching. The richness and diversity of traditional Chinese culture make it challenging to present effectively. Cooperative learning encourages students to explore cultural issues from different perspectives and share their findings with peers. This increases classroom interaction and engagement, fostering a deeper understanding and appreciation of traditional Chinese culture (Zhou & Wang, 2019). For schools, adopting cooperative learning methods in traditional Chinese culture education significantly enhances teaching quality and institutional reputation. Innovative teaching methods and a focus on cultural diversity attract high-quality students and teachers, improving overall competitiveness in the educational market. Cooperative learning promotes interdisciplinary and cross-cultural communication among students and faculty, benefiting personal and professional development (Liu & Li, 2020).

Cooperative learning helps schools promote social harmony and cultural diversity. As a multi-ethnic country with rich cultural traditions. Schools help students appreciate and respect cultural differences, fostering inclusive and open-minded attitudes, and contributing to the construction of a harmonious and culturally diverse society (Li & Liu, 2021). From a governmental perspective, promoting cooperative learning methods in traditional Chinese culture education aids in cultural heritage preservation and soft power enhancement. By advancing traditional culture education, the government protects and promotes China's rich cultural heritage, strengthening its soft power on the global stage. Cooperative learning encourages innovation and creativity among young people, crucial for China's future development and competitiveness (Zhu et al., 2021). By fostering mutual understanding and communication among different ethnic groups and regions, traditional culture education helps build a more cohesive and harmonious society (Lu & Zhang, 2022).

In conclusion, applying cooperative learning methods in traditional Chinese culture education brings extensive benefits to teachers, schools, and society. It promotes innovative teaching strategies, enhances cultural diversity, supports social harmony, preserves cultural heritage, and strengthens national soft power.

1.3 Problem Statement

1.3.1 Current Challenges in Traditional Culture Education

At present, traditional culture education in colleges and universities encounters several challenges. Although its significance is widely acknowledged, a range of factors impede its successful implementation.

Lack of Student Motivation: Students lack motivation to learn about traditional culture. In modern society, the decline of traditional culture and the influence of internet culture have led to a decrease in students' interest in traditional culture. Many students perceive traditional culture as outdated and irrelevant to their current lives and future careers.

Limited Knowledge Base: Students have a limited knowledge base of traditional culture. Luo and Liu (2019) found that although 98.8% of students acknowledge the importance of traditional culture for China's development, only 39.5% feel they know or understand some of the content. Most students lack knowledge about ancient Chinese thinkers, literary masterpieces, traditional festivals, and historical events. This knowledge gap is partly due to the insufficient emphasis on traditional culture education in the higher education curriculum.

Unconducive Learning Environment: The learning environment for traditional culture education is unconducive. Traditional culture education is often limited to literary and artistic activities such as performances, calligraphy, and music, neglecting deeper philosophical and ethical teachings. The current teaching methods place too much emphasis on rote memorization and passive learning, which results in a lack of student engagement and does little to cultivate their critical thinking abilities.

Inadequate Teacher Qualifications: Inadequate teacher qualifications pose a significant challenge. Many teachers lack the necessary expertise in traditional Chinese culture and continue to use outdated teaching methods. This issue is particularly pronounced in science and engineering colleges, where traditional culture education is even more deficient compared to majors related to Chinese philosophy, history, and literature.

Disconnection from Students' Daily Lives: Traditional culture education is disconnected from students' daily lives. Research indicates that traditional culture education in colleges has become separated from students' everyday experiences, with inadequate educational content, methods, and coverage. Chi and Xu (2018) highlighted that traditional culture education in private colleges suffers from a lack of experiential learning and inadequate educational content, resulting in only 25% of students feeling that traditional culture education meets their learning needs.

1.3.2 Limitations of Traditional Teaching Methods and Ignoring Teacher Diversity

Outdated Teaching Methods: Traditional Chinese culture education primarily relies on direct instruction methods, where the teacher is the main source of knowledge and students passively receive information. This lecture-based approach often focuses on rote memorization and repetitive learning, resulting in dull content that lacks student interest and motivation. Outdated teaching methods not only fail to inspire students but also limit the development of their critical thinking and problem-solving skills (Chi & Xu, 2018; Shi, 2021).

Limited Student Engagement: Traditional teaching methods emphasize the authority of the teacher, offering limited opportunities for student interaction and engagement. In the classroom, students are typically expected to take notes, ask occasional questions, and complete assignments or exams based on the lectures. This one-way transfer of knowledge neglects active student participation, failing to fully engage students in the learning process. A lack of interactive teaching environments often leads to passive learning and limited retention of information (Chi & Xu, 2018; Shi, 2021).

Ignoring Teacher Diversity: Traditional teaching methods also overlook the diversity of teachers' backgrounds and teaching styles. Each teacher brings unique life, study, and work experiences that shape their educational views and teaching methods. However, traditional methods often standardize teaching practices, failing to leverage the diverse perspectives and methods that different teachers can offer (Chi & Xu, 2018; Shi, 2021). This uniformity in teaching approaches limits the potential for more dynamic and varied instructional methods that could cater to the diverse needs and learning styles of students.

Teacher-Centered Approach: Traditional teaching methods are predominantly teacher-centered, which can marginalize the student's role in the learning process. Teachers often dominate the classroom, focusing on knowledge transmission rather than fostering a more interactive and student-centered learning environment. This teacher-dominated model highlights the teacher's status and role, making students passive recipients of information, which can stifle their initiative and autonomy in learning (Shi, 2021). Even though some excellent teachers may attempt to involve students more actively, such efforts are often limited and conditional.

1.3.3 Innovative Teaching Methods and the Potential of Cooperative Learning

1. Innovative Teaching Methods

To address the limitations of traditional teaching methods, many scholars have proposed innovative teaching approaches to enhance the effectiveness of Chinese traditional culture education. Project-Based Learning is a student-centered approach that emphasizes active learning and problem-solving. It encourages students to collaborate on projects related to Chinese traditional culture, thereby enhancing their understanding of the subject. Chen and Yu (2019) found that project-based learning significantly improved students' comprehension of traditional culture, communication, and collaboration skills, as well as fostering creativity.

Experiential Learning focuses on learning through direct experience. Students engage in activities such as calligraphy, painting, and tea ceremonies to immerse themselves in Chinese traditional culture. According to Li and Ma (2018), experiential learning helps students gain a deeper understanding of traditional culture, enhances their appreciation of its beauty, and strengthens their emotional connection to it. Gamification incorporates game elements such as rewards, competition, and challenges into the learning process, making it more engaging and interactive. Zhang and Li (2020) demonstrated that gamification effectively increases students' interest in learning traditional culture and improves learning outcomes.

2. The Potential of Cooperative Learning

Cooperative learning, which emphasizes group work and collaboration among students, has shown great potential in enhancing the teaching effectiveness of Chinese traditional culture courses.

Enhancing Cultural Understanding and Appreciation: Cooperative learning facilitates deeper understanding of Chinese traditional culture through peer discussions and collaborative learning. Zhang and Li (2021) found that cooperative learning not only improved students' comprehension of traditional culture but also promoted appreciation of its significance by exposing students to diverse perspectives.

Promoting Communication and Interpersonal Skills: Traditional Chinese culture education emphasizes the importance of interpersonal relationships and communication skills. Cooperative learning provides a platform for students to practice and develop these skills. Wang and Zhang (2021) reported that cooperative learning significantly enhanced students' communication, collaboration, and social skills in the context of traditional culture education.

Improving Learning Outcomes and Motivation: Chen and Huang (2020) found that cooperative learning significantly improved academic achievement in Chinese traditional culture courses compared to traditional lecture-based methods. Cooperative learning also fosters a positive and supportive learning environment, boosting students' motivation and engagement.

Despite the significant potential of cooperative learning in Chinese traditional culture education, its implementation faces challenges. The traditional hierarchical culture in China may hinder the effectiveness of cooperative learning, as students might be reluctant to express their opinions or challenge peers due to cultural norms. Additionally, the lack of appropriate assessment and evaluation methods may limit the effectiveness of cooperative learning. Therefore, it is crucial to develop suitable evaluation methods to measure the effectiveness of cooperative learning in this context.

1.3.4 Necessity and Research Gaps of TCC& CLM

Traditional Chinese culture education often lacks relevance to students' daily lives and fails to meet their learning needs. Surveys indicate that only 25% of students believe traditional culture education meets their needs, 50% think it is average, and 25% find it unsatisfactory (Chi & Xu, 2018). Additionally, traditional teaching methods rely heavily on lectures and rote memorization, ignoring students' active roles and initiatives, which fails to stimulate students' interest and motivation (Yan, 2020). The neglect of teacher diversity is also a significant issue. Teachers come from various backgrounds with different life, study, and work experiences that shape their educational perspectives and teaching methods. However, traditional teaching methods often standardize teaching practices, failing to leverage the diverse perspectives and methods different teachers can offer (Zhou, Liu, & Wang, 2014). This uniformity limits the flexibility and innovation in teaching, preventing the accommodation of diverse student needs and learning styles.

Therefore, it is crucial to reform traditional Chinese culture education methods to enhance teaching effectiveness and make it more relevant and meaningful. Integrating modern educational technologies and innovative teaching methods, such as project-based learning, experiential learning, and gamification, can create a more comprehensive and interactive learning environment, increasing student engagement and learning outcomes (Chen & Yu, 2019; Li & Ma, 2018; Zhang & Li, 2020).

Despite the demonstrated effectiveness of cooperative learning in improving students' academic achievement, motivation, and social skills, there is a relative scarcity of research on its application in Chinese traditional culture education. Most existing studies focus on primary education and English writing instruction, with few examining its use in higher education, particularly in traditional culture courses (Chen & Huang, 2020). Current research primarily addresses the impact of culture on learning outcomes or explores specific historical aspects, without fully considering the potential benefits of cooperative learning (Chen & Huang, 2020). This research gap limits the development of tailored cooperative learning strategies for traditional culture education and impedes a comprehensive understanding of its effects on student motivation, performance, and engagement.

This study aims to fill this research gap by exploring effective strategies for teaching Chinese traditional culture within a cooperative learning framework. By drawing on relevant theories such as Vygotsky's sociocultural theory, constructivist theory, humanistic theory, group dynamics theory, and social interdependence theory, this research will investigate how cooperative learning can enhance students' engagement, cultural understanding, and learning outcomes in traditional culture education (Vygotsky, 1978; Johnson & Johnson, 2009). The findings will contribute to our understanding of how to optimally utilize cooperative learning to teach Chinese traditional culture and provide guidance for developing effective teaching practices in this area.

CHAPTER TWO

LITERATURE REVIEW

2.1 Introduction

This chapter aims to provide a comprehensive literature review on cooperative learning and its application in Chinese traditional culture education. It begins by defining the concepts of cooperative learning and Chinese traditional culture and reviewing the current state of research on cooperative learning in both Chinese and international contexts. Additionally, the chapter examines the theoretical underpinnings of cooperative learning, including the social construction, humanism, group dynamics and social dependence theory. The following sections of the chapter focus on the role of previous research in improving student performance, motivation, and social skills, as well as summarizing the five key elements of cooperative learning and the role of teachers in facilitating cooperative learning activities.

2.2 Theoretical basis of cooperative learning

2.2.1 Social Constructivism Theory

Social Constructivism Theory (SCT) was proposed and developed primarily by Soviet psychologist Lev Vygotsky in the 1920s and 1930s (Vygotsky, 1978; Vygotsky, 1986). Vygotsky's theory emphasizes that knowledge is co-constructed through social interaction and cultural context, rather than through individual exploration and discovery alone. Vygotsky's main ideas include the Zone of Proximal Development (ZPD), which refers to the range of a student's potential ability to perform tasks that he or she could not perform independently but can achieve with the assistance of a competent person. This concept underscores the cognitive level a student can attain through appropriate instruction and interaction. According to Vygotsky, learning is inherently a social process where students construct knowledge through interactions with teachers, parents, or peers. These interactions provide the necessary support and guidance to enable students to think and learn at a higher level (Vygotsky, 1978; Vygotsky, 1986).

Constructivist learning theory has universal guiding significance for teaching and constructivist learning theory has become a significant guiding force in teaching and learning in the information age (Campbell & Tran, 2023). One of the representatives of cognitive constructivism, Jean Piaget argues that knowledge acquisition should be an active process of construction rather than passive acceptance (Waite-Stupiansky, 2022). Students should be viewed as the primary actors in the learning process, and teachers should act as facilitators to guide the process of learning. With the guidance of teachers, students can consciously and actively construct knowledge. Cooperative learning, as a new type of teaching activity, is well-suited to meet the requirements of constructivist learning theory for education (Lenkauskaitė & Bubnys, 2020). Through group cooperation, students can engage in discussion and exploration in a supportive atmosphere, and the results of each group can be shared and discussed. Teachers can then provide a final summary that supplements and synthesizes the groups' insights, thereby facilitating a process of knowledge and experience reorganization that is crucial to the learning process in the classroom.

Social constructivism emphasizes that individuals construct knowledge through social interaction and cultural background, where personal experience serves as the foundation for understanding things (Amineh & Asl, 2015). In contrast to other constructivist theories, social constructivism emphasizes the importance of social aspects in the construction process. In active learning methods developed based on constructivist theories, the student plays the role of the constructor of information and takes an active role (Piaget, 1967; Vygotsky, 1978). The cooperative learning process aligns with the principles of social constructivism, where students actively construct knowledge through interaction with others Constructivism. Through the exchange of opinions, learners develop a richer understanding of concepts, which helps in the rational development of their cognitive structures (Brau, 2020).

In the practical application of constructivist teaching, several steps are typically followed (Waite-Stupiansky, 2022). Firstly, students are organized into groups and explore problems under the leadership of a group leader, establishing basic principles for cooperative learning. Secondly, the teacher poses a question to the class and students discuss it in groups, expressing their opinions and sorting out their thoughts. Thirdly, follow-up actions are taken to promote independent learning. Fourthly, students present their group's findings to the class. Finally, students reflect on their learning experience. Cooperative learning is an effective way to promote knowledge construction in the classroom, and it is important to apply it in a manner consistent with constructivist learning theory (Lenkauskaitė & Bubnys, 2020). In this approach, teachers set up enlightening questions before class, design activities that engage students and promote critical thinking, guide students' activities, and provide fair evaluation and motivation.

To facilitate effective meaning construction, teachers should leverage the conditions that are present during cooperative learning activities and provide guidance to students. Strategies for guidance may include creating an active classroom atmosphere, stimulating student interest and enthusiasm through thoughtful questions, guiding group discussions, enhancing student comprehension, and encouraging students to discover and correct their misconceptions (Erbil, 2020). This approach is supported by several studies. For example, a meta-analysis conducted by Johnson and Johnson (2009) found that cooperative learning leads to higher academic achievement, greater motivation, and better social skills among students. Additionally, a study by Niu and colleagues (2018) found that cooperative learning is effective in teaching

Chinese culture and history to university students. By emphasizing active learning and collaboration, cooperative learning promotes a constructivist approach to learning that is particularly relevant in the information age.

At the same time, several studies have shown the effectiveness of cooperative learning in promoting constructivist learning. For example, a study by Savery and Duffy (1996) found that cooperative learning promotes active learning, enhances students' critical thinking skills, and increases student motivation. Additionally, a study by Chen and colleagues (2018) found that cooperative learning was effective in promoting knowledge construction and academic achievement in primary school students. Therefore, cooperative learning can be a valuable tool for promoting constructivist learning in the classroom.

2.2.2 Humanistic Theory

Humanism is a psychological perspective that emphasizes individual freedom, human potential, and personal growth (Boeree, 2006). This theory originated in the 1940s and 1950s, primarily developed by psychologists Abraham Maslow and Carl Rogers. Maslow introduced the hierarchy of needs in his 1943 paper, "A Theory of Human Motivation," proposing that human needs are arranged in a hierarchy from physiological needs to safety, love and belonging, esteem, and self-actualization (Maslow, 1943). Rogers, in his 1951 book, "Client-Centered Therapy: Its Current Practice, Implications, and Theory," elaborated on the person-centered approach, stressing the importance of unconditional positive regard, empathy, and authenticity (Rogers, 1951). Rogers advocated for a "student-centered" teaching approach, where the teacher's role is to guide and facilitate the learning process rather than merely transmitting knowledge (Hartman, 2020). He believed that students learn best when motivated by their own interests and passions, and that teachers should create a supportive learning environment that encourages exploration and self-discovery (Boeree, 2006). In this approach, the teacher acts as a facilitator, helping students develop their potential and grow as individuals.

The humanistic theory represented by Rogers emphasizes the importance of the whole person in learning and development. Rogers believed that education should aim to develop students' moral, intellectual, physical, aesthetic, and labor abilities, as well as their ability to cooperate with others (Feigenbaum, 2024). The learning process should not only focus on acquiring essential knowledge and skills, but also on cultivating student's values, attitudes, and emotions. Rogers believed that authentic learning should be an active and participatory process where learners are engaged and motivated by their own interests and passions (Boeree, 2006). Teachers should provide students with learning resources, create a positive and supportive learning environment, and encourage students to develop their own unique strengths and abilities.

Research supports the effectiveness of humanistic teaching approaches. For example, a study by Jeong and colleagues (2016) found that humanistic teaching methods effectively improved students' motivation and academic achievement. Another study by Colucci and colleagues (2019) found that a humanistic approach to teaching effectively promoted critical thinking skills among college students.

The humanistic approach to education places a high value on individual freedom, personal growth, and the holistic development of students. This approach emphasizes creating a supportive and engaging learning environment that encourages students to discover their own potential and become lifelong learners. Rogers and Maslow, two prominent representatives of the humanistic approach, believe that authentic learning should be centered on the integrity of people and that students' learning is influenced by both internal and external factors (Feigenbaum, 2024). Therefore, teachers should focus on creating an environment that supports students' internal drive to learn independently, enhances their autonomy and enthusiasm for learning, and develops their emotional and cognitive aspects.

Cooperative learning is one teaching method that aligns with the humanistic approach by meeting the psychological needs of students. Cooperative learning in groups provides students with opportunities to collaborate and engage in active learning, which can promote their autonomy, motivation, and social skills (Johnson & Johnson, 2009). By working together in a supportive and stimulating learning environment, students can discover their own potential and develop their specialties. Additionally, cooperative learning emphasizes the importance of student-centered learning, which is a critical component of the humanistic approach to education. To summarize, the humanistic approach to education highlights the significance of establishing a nurturing and immersive learning atmosphere that fosters the comprehensive growth of students. Cooperative learning serves as a proficient instructional technique that resonates with the tenets of the humanistic approach as it addresses students' psychological requirements and encourages interactive learning within a collaborative setting.

2.2.3 Group Dynamics Theory

John Dewey proposed the idea of "democratic education" in 1916, pointing out that education should cultivate students' democratic literacy and enable them to experience the democratic process in school life, so as to prepare them for participating in social democratic life in the future. Dewey believes that education is not only about implanting knowledge, but also about cultivating students' critical thinking ability and social responsibility. Democratic education emphasizes the active participation and cooperation of students in the learning process, as well as the interaction and joint decision-making between teachers and students. This educational philosophy advocates developing students' democratic awareness and cooperative ability through practical democratic practices, such as group discussions and collaborative projects (Dewey, 1916).

Herbert Thelen further developed John Dewey's idea of "democratic education" and proposed the theory of group dynamics. The theory emphasizes the importance of groups in learning and believes that the interaction between group members can promote individual development and learning. Cooperative learning promotes the development of academic and social skills through group activities, using the principles of group dynamics to enhance cooperation and communication among students (Thelen, 1954). On this basis, the content of group dynamics theory should be described in detail and the literature should be noted. Kurt Lewin's work on group dynamics laid the foundation for understanding how individuals behave in group settings, focusing on aspects such as group processes, leadership, and group decision-making (Lewin,1947)..

The theory of group dynamics contains the following key elements:

Group Interdependence: Thelen emphasized that the interaction and interdependence among group members significantly impact group dynamics. Positive interdependence occurs when group members perceive that their success is linked to the success of their peers. This concept was further supported by Johnson and Johnson, who introduced positive, negative, and cooperative interdependence (Johnson & Johnson, 2021).

Group Motivation: Interaction and internal tensions within a group can motivate members to achieve common goals. By fostering cooperation and communication, group members can collectively overcome challenges and achieve desired learning outcomes. Bruce Tuckman's research on group development stages aligns with this view, proposing that groups move through forming, storming, norming, and performing stages to reach high performance (Tuckman, 1965).

Cooperation and Communication: Group Dynamics Theory emphasizes the importance of cooperation and communication in cooperative learning. Through group activities, students share knowledge and skills, enhancing both academic and social abilities. This aligns with Vygotsky's sociocultural theory, which stresses the role of interaction in knowledge construction (Vygotsky, 1978).

Stages of Group Development: Thelen identified stages of group development, including forming, storming, norming, and performing. Each stage has distinct group dynamics and interaction patterns. During the forming stage, group members get to know each other and establish initial relationships. The storming stage may involve conflicts and disagreements. The norming stage sees the establishment of norms and behavioral guidelines, while the performing stage involves efficient collaboration to achieve common goals (Thelen, 1954). Tuckman later added an adjourning stage, where the group disbands after task completion (Tuckman, 1977).

Task Roles and Maintenance Roles: Thelen distinguished between task roles, which focus on achieving group objectives, and maintenance roles, which aim to maintain group harmony and cohesion. The balance between these roles is crucial for group success (Thelen, 1954). Tuckman also highlighted the need for balancing task-oriented and social interactions to maintain effective cooperation (Tuckman, 1965).

Group Dynamics Theory provides a solid theoretical foundation for cooperative learning. By understanding group interaction mechanisms, educators can design more effective group activities that promote cooperation and communication among students. Cooperative learning methods, grounded in group dynamics principles, can significantly enhance students' academic performance and social skills. This approach not only aids in knowledge acquisition but also develops teamwork and social responsibility.

2.2.4 Social Interdependence Theory

In 1935, Coffka, a German-American psychologist and representative of Gestalt psychology, first proposed the concept of "group dynamic integrity." Through his research, he concluded that a group functions as a unified and dynamic entity, where the interdependence among its members can significantly fluctuate due to various factors (Ye, 2014). In 1947, Kurt further emphasized that the essence of group motivation lies in the interdependence of the "dynamic whole" (Kurt, 1947).

Following in the footsteps of his mentor Lewin, Dodge, in 1949, introduced the concept of two interdependent states within a group: positive and negative interdependence. Dodge also highlighted that when group members collectively strive for a shared goal, a team is formed, which further drives the group's dynamics. Any changes in the status of individual members or subgroups can influence other members or subgroups to adapt accordingly. Additionally, internal tensions among group members can serve as a motivating force to achieve a common objective. Social interdependence emphasizes the importance of the dynamic whole and interdependence in group motivation. Coffka argued that a group is a whole and that the whole is dynamic, constantly changing due to various factors (Ye, 2014). The Johnson brothers expanded on this theory and proposed the concept of interdependence beyond positive and negative, adding cooperative interdependence as a third type. They also identified three organizational structures for student groups: group cooperation, group competition, and individualistic efforts (Johnson & Johnson, 2021).

If the team members can work together, learn to cooperate with others, and pool their wisdom, they will get twice the result with half the effort. On the contrary, if the members compete and do not know how to communicate and share information with others, the completion of the task will be affected to a certain extent. Similarly, if everyone acted behind closed doors, it wouldn't end up very well. In cooperative learning, creating positive interdependence scenarios is essential for success. Teachers should focus on creating a supportive and engaging learning environment that fosters a sense of collective belonging, value recognition, and connection among members. Positive interdependence encourages members to help each other and rely on each other, leading to mutual growth and win-win outcomes. Cooperative learning also cultivates students' sense of self-responsibility and communication skills, making it a crucial factor in education (Roger & Johnson, 1994).

In the classroom teaching of traditional Chinese culture, students should not win or lose but live in harmonious coexistence. If the success of others represents their own failure, then the competition between peers will become more and more intense; positive and friendly competition is what everyone wants to see, but also can improve each other's ability. Therefore, it is necessary for active mutual dependence in class, especially important for primary school students. Primary school students study habits, personality, emotions, and cognitive levels are in the formative period, the positive mutual dependence lets students learn to rely on others, and trust others.

Social interdependence theory helps teachers focus more on creating positive interdependence scenarios when designing collaborative learning. For example, let participants like their team, help participants find a sense of collective belonging, feel their value is recognized and affirmed, let members connect to each other, promote their mutual growth, and achieve win-win results.

Group members help each other, rely on each other, and make progress with each other. Each student can feel the collective power of the group. In the process of getting along with others, they also cultivate the students' sense of self-responsibility and learn to be responsible for others and themselves. At the same time, communication between the members also improves the students' communication skills to a certain extent, which are all the necessary factors that constitute cooperative learning and play a crucial role in cooperative learning. The social interdependence theory serves as a fundamental framework for comprehending the significance of group motivation and interdependence within the context of cooperative learning. By establishing a positive interdependence scenario, educators can effectively cultivate a supportive and captivating learning environment that fosters individual progress and the holistic development of students. In traditional Chinese culture, the emphasis on harmonious coexistence and positive and friendly competition aligns with the principles of positive interdependence. For students, who are in the formative period of their study habits, personality, emotion, and cognitive development, active mutual dependence is especially important. It helps them learn to rely on and trust others, and promotes emotional and cognitive development (Chen, 2017).

2.3 Traditional Direct Instruction Approach

2.3.1 Teaching method

Traditional direct instruction methods refer to the instructional techniques and practices that have been used for centuries to transmit knowledge and skills from teachers to students. These methods are typically characterized by a lecture-based approach in which the teacher is the primary source of information and knowledge, and the students are expected to listen, take notes, and memorize the information presented to them (Shirley & Irani, 2020).

In traditional direct instruction methods, the focus is on the teacher as the primary authority figure in the classroom, with the teacher taking a central role in the transmission of knowledge. This approach to teaching has been criticized for being overly teacher-centered and for limiting student engagement and critical thinking. (Ghaleb, 2024). However, traditional teaching methods have been used successfully for centuries and continue to be used in many educational settings around the world (Wu & Yang, 2020).

Despite the criticisms of traditional direct instruction methods, there are still advantages to this approach. Traditional teaching methods can be effective in delivering information and building foundational knowledge (Nisar & Hussain, 2023). Moreover, traditional direct instruction methods can be particularly useful for large classes, where a lecture-based approach may be more efficient than other teaching approaches (Shirley & Irani, 2020).

2.3.2 Teaching practice

Traditional Chinese culture education often relies on a lecture-based approach, where the teacher is the primary source of knowledge and information. In this method, the teacher delivers lectures on topics related to Chinese culture, history, and philosophy, while students are expected to listen attentively, take notes, and memorize the material presented.

The use of lecture-based instruction in traditional Chinese culture teaching can be traced back to Confucianism, which emphasizes the importance of education and the role of the teacher in transmitting knowledge and moral values to students (Hao, 2017). In this approach, the teacher is seen as a mentor and guide, responsible for imparting knowledge, developing the student's character, and cultivating their moral values. While lecture-based instruction has been criticized for being overly teacher-centered and limiting student engagement and critical thinking (Shafi & Masood, 2023), it remains a prevalent teaching method in traditional Chinese culture. This approach is particularly suited to transmitting foundational knowledge and building a shared understanding of cultural values and traditions (Wu & Yang, 2020). In addition to lectures, traditional direct instruction methods in Chinese culture also include the use of textbooks, which serve as a key source of information for students (Zhang & Wang, 2019). These textbooks are carefully curated to ensure that they accurately reflect the cultural values and traditions of Chinese society. Moreover, the content of Chinese traditional culture courses in China often focuses on historical events, literature, and art, while ignoring the practical application of Chinese traditional culture in modern society (Wang, 2019). This approach to education may not be relevant to the needs of students in the modern world and may not help them to understand and appreciate the value of Chinese traditional culture.

According to research by Wang (2023), traditional Chinese culture views education as a means of cultivating moral character and developing practical skills that can be applied in everyday life. As such, the teacher is viewed as an authority figure, and students are expected to respect their authority. Classroom discipline is emphasized, and students are expected to be attentive and well-behaved. One teaching practice that is commonly used in traditional Chinese culture teaching is the use of memorization. Students are expected to memorize a large amount of information, including historical events, literary works, and cultural values. This is viewed as an important aspect of learning, as it helps to develop a strong foundation of knowledge that can be built upon in future studies (Huang, 2019). Furthermore, the use of storytelling is also common in traditional Chinese culture teaching. Stories are used to convey important moral lessons and cultural values and are often used as a means of engaging students and promoting their interest in the topic being taught (Zhang, 2016).

In traditional Chinese culture teaching, rote learning is seen as a useful technique to reinforce learning and develop memory skills. According to a study by Xie et al. (2018), rote learning is considered an effective method of learning in Chinese culture due to the emphasis on memorization and repetition in Confucianism. Rote learning is used to memorize poetry, historical dates, and other important information. However, critics of this approach argue that it may lead to superficial learning and limit students' ability to develop critical thinking skills (Liu, 2013).

The materials used in traditional Chinese culture teaching are varied and include textbooks, historical documents, poetry, and artwork. Textbooks provide students with comprehensive knowledge of the topic being taught. Historical documents are used to provide students with a deeper understanding of the historical context of the topic, and they are often analyzed in detail in class to develop critical thinking skills. Poetry and artwork are used to provide students with a more nuanced understanding of the cultural values and aesthetic traditions of traditional Chinese culture (Tang, 2018).

Additionally, calligraphy is also a significant element in traditional Chinese culture teaching, as it is seen as an art form that embodies the cultural values of patience, discipline, and concentration (Xu & Li, 2018). Students are often taught to write characters using traditional brush and ink techniques, which require a great deal of practice and skill development.

2.3.3 Teaching evaluation

Evaluation is an important aspect of education that helps measure students' knowledge and skills in each subject. In traditional Chinese culture teaching, evaluation methods are typically focused on testing students' knowledge and understanding of the material presented in the classroom. These methods include written exams, oral exams, and essays (Zhao, 2018). Written exams are typically used to evaluate students' ability to memorize and recall information presented in the classroom. Oral exams are used to evaluate students' ability to articulate their understanding of the material, while essays are used to evaluate students' ability to express their ideas in a written format. Therefore, Evaluation and assessment of Chinese traditional culture courses in China is another area that needs improvement. Currently, most Chinese traditional culture courses are evaluated based on student feedback and grades, which may not accurately reflect the effectiveness of the curriculum (Liu, 2021). There is a need for more comprehensive and valid evaluation methods to assess the impact of Chinese traditional culture education on students' knowledge, skills, and attitudes.

Assessment methods in traditional Chinese culture teaching often rely on memorization and recall, with students being tested on their ability to memorize and recite key facts and information (Zhang & Wang, 2019). This approach is consistent with the emphasis on rote learning and memorization in traditional Chinese education, which is viewed as essential for developing a strong foundation of knowledge (Hao, 2017). According to research by Cheng and Wang (2019), traditional Chinese culture places a high value on academic achievement and success, and as such, assessments often emphasize the importance of memorization and recall of information.

In recent years, there has been a growing trend towards the use of performance-based evaluation methods in traditional Chinese culture teaching. Performance-based evaluation methods focus on evaluating students' ability to apply the knowledge and skills they have gained in the classroom to real-world situations. This approach emphasizes the application of knowledge and skills, rather than just memorization and recall (Wang & Li, 2018). There is a growing trend towards the use of performance-based evaluation methods, which emphasize the application of knowledge and skills to real-world situations.

In conclusion, traditional direct instruction methods remain prominent in traditional Chinese culture teaching. These methods place an emphasis on the transfer of knowledge from the teacher to the student, with a focus on memorization and the development of critical thinking skills. The use of textbooks, historical documents, poetry, and artwork provides students with a comprehensive understanding of the topic being taught. The evaluation methods used in traditional Chinese culture teaching typically include written exams, oral exams, and essays, which test students' knowledge and comprehension of the material. However, there has been a recent trend towards the incorporation of performance-based evaluation methods, which assess students' ability to apply the knowledge and skills they have learned to real-world scenarios.

It is important to note that traditional direct instruction methods and materials are deeply rooted in the cultural heritage and historical development of Chinese education. As such, they continue to play a significant role in the education system in China and in the teaching of traditional Chinese culture globally. However, as education systems evolve and adapt to changing societal needs and technological advancements, there is also a growing interest in exploring new teaching methods and innovative approaches that can enhance the learning experience for students. Although traditional teaching methods and materials remain important in traditional Chinese culture teaching, there is also a need to adapt to changing educational environments and incorporate new approaches to meet the evolving needs of students.

2.4 Cooperative Learning Approach

2.4.1 The definition of cooperative learning

Cooperative learning, also known as group learning, originated in the 18th century in the UK and spread to the US in the 19th century. In the 1970s, American scholar David Koonts advocated for the application of cooperative learning strategies in education (He, 2012). Today, cooperative learning is widely used globally.

Cooperative learning is a student-centered instructional strategy where students work in small groups to explore, discuss, and learn. This approach transforms passive learning into active learning, stimulating students' interest and encouraging them to acquire knowledge and develop inquiry skills (Sun & Wang, 2004). Cooperative learning also enhances communication between teachers and students, fosters healthy psychological development, and improves the learning environment (Sun & Wang, 2004).

Although various definitions of cooperative learning exist, the core idea is the same: achieving learning goals through group cooperation. Sharon (1976) described cooperative learning as an umbrella term for classroom teaching that involves organizing and collaborating within the classroom. Slavin (2013) described it as a new teaching strategy where teachers guide students who are divided into small groups to help each other, learn together, and complete tasks. Teachers then reward students based on their performance (Johnson & Johnson, 2008).

According to Johnson and Johnson (2008), cooperative learning comprises five essential elements (Johnson & Johnson, 2008; Yassin et al., 2018):

1. Positive Interdependence:

Students believe they need each other to achieve their goals. Each member's success depends on the collective effort, which can be ensured by assigning specific roles or tasks (Johnson & Johnson, 2008).

2. Individual Accountability:

Each student must contribute to the group's success and be accountable for their own learning. This prevents "free riding" and can be reinforced through individual and group assessments (Johnson & Johnson, 2008; Yassin et al., 2018).

3. Face-to-Face Promotive Interaction:

Group members interact directly, supporting and encouraging each other. This interaction helps complete academic tasks and fosters social connections and trust (Johnson & Johnson, 2008).

4. Social Skills:

Students develop and practice communication, leadership, decision-making, and conflict-resolution skills. These essential skills for effective collaboration can be cultivated through teacher guidance and group activities (Johnson & Johnson, 2008).

5. Group Processing:

Students reflect on group effectiveness, identifying strengths and areas for improvement. Regular reflection and feedback help optimize group interactions and enhance overall group efficiency (Johnson & Johnson, 2008; Yassin et al., 2018).

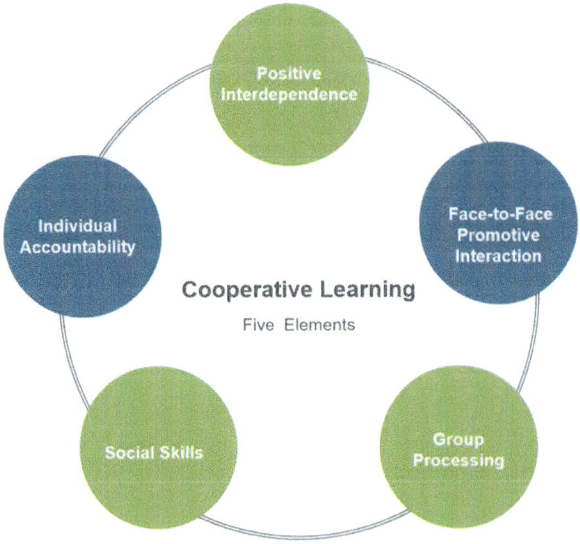

FIGURE 2.1: Cooperative Learning Five Elements Graph

Erbil (2020) emphasizes that effective collaboration and problem-solving are the primary goals of cooperative learning. Group members work towards common objectives, and teachers evaluate individual contributions and use effective reward mechanisms (Erbil, 2020). Radjabova (2023) notes that cooperative learning groups should be heterogeneous within and homogeneous between groups to facilitate mutual help and problem-solving within the group.

While scholars have various interpretations of cooperative learning, they commonly understand it as an approach where students work in heterogeneous groups under teacher guidance. Each member participates and cooperates to complete tasks, with group performance being a key evaluation and reward criterion. This method not only helps students acquire knowledge but also serves as an effective teaching strategy for educators. Teachers must understand their students well, group them based on their characteristics and abilities, provide platforms for communication, and establish evaluation measures (Radjabova, 2023).

By integrating these fundamental elements, cooperative learning effectively enhances academic performance, social skills, and motivation, promoting positive interaction and cooperation among students. This instructional strategy not only aids in knowledge acquisition but also develops students' overall abilities, laying a solid foundation for their future development (Johnson & Johnson, 2008; Millis, 2023; Sharon, 1976; Slavin, 2013).

2.4.2 Implementation of Cooperative Learning

There are various methods to implement cooperative learning in the classroom. Below are several common cooperative learning strategies, detailing the roles of students and teachers, as well as group formation and organization:

1. **Jigsaw Method**

The Jigsaw Method is an effective cooperative learning strategy where students are divided into small groups, and each member is responsible for learning a subtopic. They then return to their original group to teach their peers. The teacher's role is to assign subtopics, provide resources, and monitor group discussions. The students' role is to actively participate, learn, and teach the subtopic, ensuring everyone understands the entire topic. Groups are typically heterogeneous to maximize diverse perspectives and skills (Aronson, 1978).

2. Think-Pair-Share

Think-Pair-Share is a simple yet powerful technique that encourages individual and collaborative thinking. Students first contemplate a question or problem independently, then pair up with a partner to discuss their thoughts, and finally share with the entire class. The teacher's role is to pose the question, provide thinking time, and facilitate the class discussion. The students' role is to think independently, share ideas with a partner, and contribute to the class discussion. This method works well with both homogeneous and heterogeneous groupings (Lyman, 1981).

3.Round-Robin Brainstorming

In Round-Robin Brainstorming, students take turns speaking within their group, ensuring equal participation. This method can be used to generate ideas, solve problems, or discuss topics. The teacher's role is to set the question or task and ensure each student has the opportunity to speak. The students' role is to share their thoughts in turn, listen to others, and contribute ideas. Groups are usually formed to ensure a mix of abilities and backgrounds (Kagan, 1992).

3. Group Investigation

Group Investigation involves students working together to select, research, and present a topic. This strategy typically includes phases such as topic selection, planning, research, presentation, and evaluation. The teacher's role is to offer topic choices, guide the research process, and evaluate the presentations. The students' role is to collaborate in planning and conducting the research, synthesizing information, and presenting their findings. Groups are typically heterogeneous to leverage diverse skills and knowledge (Sharan & Sharan, 1992).

4. **Peer Tutoring**

Peer Tutoring pairs students so that one student helps another learn a concept or skill. This method benefits both the tutor and the tutee, as the tutor reinforces their own understanding while the tutee receives personalized instruction. The teacher's role is to pair students appropriately, provide tutoring materials, and monitor the tutoring sessions. The students' role is to participate as tutors or tutees, helping each other understand and master the learning content. Groupings can be homogeneous or heterogeneous depending on the skill being taught (Topping, 1996).

5. **Collaborative Writing**

Collaborative Writing involves students working together to produce a written document. Each member contributes to planning, drafting, and revising the text. The teacher's role is to set the writing task, provide guidance and feedback, and evaluate the final product. The students' role is to collaborate on planning, writing, and editing the text, ensuring the final product reflects the group's collective effort. Groups are often heterogeneous to combine different writing strengths and perspectives (Ede & Lunsford, 1990).

2.4.3 Theoretical and Empirical research on cooperative learning

1. **Research on cooperative learning abroad**

Cooperative learning is an effective teaching method that has been widely studied and applied in educational settings. It involves students working together in small groups to achieve a common goal, while also developing social skills and positive interdependence. In this literature review, we will examine the research on cooperative learning in different countries and contexts, including its benefits, challenges, and applications.

Benefits of Cooperative Learning numerous studies have shown that cooperative learning has many benefits for students. One of the main benefits is improved academic performance. For example, a meta-analysis by Johnson, Johnson, and Miguel, et al. (2023) found that cooperative learning had a positive effect on academic achievement across different subjects and age groups. Another benefit is the development of social and emotional skills, such as communication, teamwork, and empathy (Kagan, 1992; Slavin, 1987). Additionally, cooperative learning has been shown to improve motivation, engagement, and self-esteem (Agwu & Nmadu, 2023).

Despite the advantages of cooperative learning, it faces several challenges. A significant issue is the presence of free-riders, individuals who contribute less to the group effort, undermining the collective work (Tamimy et al., 2023). Equally challenging is maintaining a balance between individual accountability and group success; students are expected to be responsible for their own learning while contributing effectively to the group's objectives (Yeh, 2023). Additionally, cooperative learning can be particularly challenging for students who experience social anxiety or find group activities difficult, as these issues may limit their engagement in such learning methods (Millis, 2023).

Cooperative learning has been applied in various educational settings and contexts around the world (Dyson, et.al, 2022). In the United States, cooperative learning has been widely used in K-12 classrooms, with many teachers using structured group work activities to improve student learning and social skills (Moore & Corter, 2022). In Europe, cooperative learning has been applied in higher education to improve student engagement and critical thinking skills (Johnson & Johnson, 2009).

In recent years, there has also been a growing interest in the application of cooperative learning in online and hybrid learning environments. For example, A study by Gürbüz and Karamete (2020) investigated the effectiveness of cooperative learning on students' academic achievement in science education. The results of the study showed that students who participated in cooperative learning groups had significantly higher academic achievement scores compared to those who learned individually.

Baydas and Genc (2021) found that cooperative learning had a positive impact on students' attitudes towards science, with students in the cooperative learning group showing greater interest in science and higher levels of engagement. Azizi and Rastegar (2020) investigated the effect of cooperative learning on the development of critical thinking skills in EFL learners and found that it had a positive effect on the development of critical thinking skills in EFL learners, especially in the areas of analysis, evaluation, and inference. Neri and Miri (2020) explored the impact of cooperative learning on students' creativity in science education and found that it had a significant positive effect on students' creativity in science, with students in the cooperative learning group demonstrating higher levels of originality, fluency, and flexibility in their thinking. DeRoche and Kellogg (2019) investigated the impact of cooperative learning on student motivation and engagement in online courses and found that students who participated in cooperative learning activities had higher levels of motivation and engagement compared to those who learned individually.

These studies suggest that cooperative learning can have a positive impact on students' attitudes towards learning, development of critical thinking skills, creativity, and motivation and engagement in learning. These findings are consistent with previous research conducted in China and other countries, which indicates the effectiveness of cooperative learning in promoting student learning and achievement.

Overall, cooperative learning has been extensively studied and applied in different countries and contexts. The above studies suggest that cooperative learning can have a positive impact on students' attitudes towards learning, development of critical thinking skills, creativity, and motivation and engagement in learning. However, it also poses challenges such as free-riders, individual and group accountability, and social anxiety. Despite these challenges, cooperative learning has been successfully applied in various educational settings, including K-12 classrooms, traditional classrooms, and higher education. With the increasing use of online and hybrid learning environments, there is also a growing interest in the application of cooperative learning in these contexts.

2. Research on Cooperative Learning in China

Cooperative learning, a teaching method developed in the 1970s and 1980s, has shown great effectiveness in improving the classroom environment, enhancing academic performance, and fostering positive qualities in students. It quickly gained global recognition and became a popular teaching approach, often considered the most significant and successful educational reform in recent years. Since the early 1990s, cooperative learning research and experiments have also emerged in China, yielding significant achievements (Gao & Zhao, 2022).

A search of domestic literature revealed that there are 4 doctoral dissertations with cooperative study as the main content, around 1,000 master's theses, and more than 95% of the research is for middle school and elementary school. There are more than 5,000 research studies about cooperative learning in the journal category. The subjects used in university education are mainly university English, and about 300 people have conducted related research on this topic (China Knowledge Network, 2022).

Over two thousand years ago, the Confucian school in China already recognized the value of cooperative learning in education. In one of the earliest books on education called "Xue Ji," it was mentioned that learning alone without friends is a lonely and uninformed experience. In the 1990s, China started incorporating foreign theories and research on cooperative learning into its teaching practices. Chinese educators also extensively analyzed cooperative learning and produced numerous writings on the subject. As representative of the pioneers of group cooperative learning, Sheng and other researches (1997) the topic of “Personality Optimization Education”, and the research time is up to 6 years. Wang and his colleagues (1993) implement "Cooperative Teaching Research and Experiments." In the experimental results, Wang Tan points out in group cooperative learning, students participate in classroom learning more actively; students have a stronger sense of teamwork; students' social skills have been greatly developed. Pei (1999) mentions in the article "Research on Developmental Teaching and Student Subjective Development" that the comprehensive literacy of students will be greatly improved when students actively participate in cooperative learning, and their cooperative ability and development will also be improved. Gao & Zhao (2022) explained the concept, principles, methods and suggestions of the cooperative learning method.

Xinjia et al. (2021) mentioned the concept of cooperative education when discussing the value of Xingzhi's life education concept in the new era. They believe that students in different classes or grades can form a learning community with common interests or research topics and carry out cooperative learning. Wang Hongyu believes that cooperative learning is a teaching strategy system. Students learn together in heterogeneous groups according to relevant procedures and methods, and cultivate cognition and emotion in cooperative interpersonal communication. "Basic Education Curriculum Reform Outline (Trial)" emphasizes that students' previous learning methods should be changed, and inquiry-based learning, autonomous learning and cooperative learning should be implemented. Zhang (2019) pointed out that cooperative learning allows students to discuss and analyze the knowledge they have learned together as to promote common development and progress. The Decision of the State Council on the Reform and Development of Basic Education (State Council, 2001) emphasizes that cooperative learning can achieve mutual learning in teaching and allow students to develop through exchanges. Guo (2016) believes that the effective application of cooperative learning in ideological and political courses can improve students' innovative ability and facilitate the interaction and cooperation between students. Students' thinking and understanding of ideological and political courses will cultivate more aspiring young people. Lu (2019) analyzed the importance of cooperative learning in teaching from the perspective of game theory. In addition to allowing students to maximize their own interests in cooperation, cooperative learning can also cultivate the core literacy of political subjects.

Wang (2023) focuses on the impact of cooperative learning on students' knowledge sharing. The study found that cooperative learning has an important impact on the recognition of interpersonal relationships and basic orientation on knowledge sharing, and enhanced students' cognition of procedural fairness, sense of belonging and willingness to share knowledge, while knowledge sharing can significantly affect the learning results. Wang (2013) believes that in the late 1990s, cooperative learning theory begin to be truly valued by the academic community, and many research results are introduced, and cooperative learning teaching research is officially on track. Gao & Zhao (2022) believes that group cooperation strategies mainly include five aspects: strengthening theoretical study and ability training, scientifically dividing cooperative study groups, setting themes and questions rationally, optimizing the implementation process guidance strategy, and establishing a sound evaluation mechanism.

Cooperative learning has effectively highlighted the main body position of students in teaching activities, enhanced students' awareness of active participation, and achieved relatively remarkable results in teaching practice (Li, 2021). Song (2021) found that in the teaching of operation research, the teaching method of cooperative learning is expected to promote communication and discussion between students, trigger a deeper thinking and exploration of the knowledge learned, improve students' ability to solve complex problems, and truly internalize the knowledge. However, whether cooperative learning can achieve the above teaching effect largely depends on teachers' understanding and overall design of cooperative learning.

Studies show that cooperative learning is of great help to students' English writing. It can relieve students' anxiety about writing and help students solve problems with writing difficulties. It improves students' language skills and writing strategies and promotes the realization of the three functions of language output. Jiafu and Jiang (2015) propose that the best grouping method is to control the number of people to 4-

6. The teacher can control the number of groups according to the actual situation. At the same time, students with different personalities and grades should be assigned to the group. Teachers lead students in cooperative learning. If the grouping strategy is implemented properly, the learning efficiency will be improved. Yang (2024) believes that the implementation of cooperative learning in high school language teaching is conducive to students' initiative. Faced with different reading themes, students will collect information, find problems, and solve problems.

Wang et al. (2021) found that cooperative learning was effective in improving students' academic achievement, with students in the cooperative learning group outperforming those in the traditional learning group. Similarly, Li et al. (2020) found that cooperative learning improved students' learning outcomes, with students in the cooperative learning group showing higher levels of understanding, retention, and transfer of knowledge.

Another study by Liu et al. (2020) investigated the impact of cooperative learning on students' social-emotional learning (SEL) outcomes. The results showed that cooperative learning was effective in improving students' SEL outcomes, including self-awareness, social awareness, self-management, relationship skills, and responsible decision-making.

A study by Song et al. (2020) examined the effect of cooperative learning on students' motivation and engagement in physical education. The results showed that cooperative learning had a positive effect on student's motivation and engagement in physical education, with students in the cooperative learning group showing higher levels of interest, enjoyment, and effort in their physical education classes. Xie and Wu (2019) explored the effect of cooperative learning on students' English writing skills. The results showed that cooperative learning was effective in improving students' English writing skills, with students in the cooperative learning group demonstrating higher levels of writing proficiency and creativity.

Based on the previous studies on cooperative learning in both domestic and international contexts, it is evident that the cooperative learning mode has been increasingly studied by scholars in recent years. The experimental research on cooperative learning by frontline teachers has contributed to the enrichment of cooperative learning theory. Moreover, cooperative learning has the potential to effectively address the current challenges in Traditional Chinese Culture education. However, it is important to note that most existing research focuses on applying cooperative learning to English writing teaching, with the main stage of the research being elementary and junior middle schools. In contrast, there are relatively few research results on cooperative learning in university-level education. Furthermore, there is a research gap in the application of cooperative learning in Chinese traditional culture and education. Therefore, it is necessary to explore the strategies and methods of Chinese Culture education based on the cooperative learning theory, in light of the new situation.

In conclusion, cooperative learning has become an increasingly popular teaching method and has shown positive effects on various aspects of education, such as academic achievement, attitude toward learning, and critical thinking skills. While most studies have focused on English writing teaching, there is a need to expand the scope of research to other areas, such as traditional Chinese culture education. By combining the cooperative learning theory with Chinese culture education, educators can explore effective strategies to cultivate students' creativity, critical thinking skills, and intercultural competence.

3. Cooperative learning and student achievement

According to a study conducted by Lu (2021), the integration of group cooperative learning into literature and language teaching has yielded positive results. Over a period of six years, the teaching outcomes have consistently improved, offering valuable insights on overcoming challenges in language instruction and maximizing the benefits of group cooperative learning in literature and language classes. The results of Yu (2020)'s English cooperative learning and teaching experiment showed that the average English score in the experimental class was 20.425 points higher than the previous test; the English post-test score was 70.87 in the experimental class, while the control class was 51.66, and the experimental class was 19.21 points higher than the control class. Research results show that the group cooperative learning method does have a positive effect on the English performance of students who are stuck in school.

Through experimental comparison, Li (2020) tested that the application of cooperative learning pedagogy in martial arts general classes had a superior impact on students' ability to cooperate, martial arts special quality, martial arts special skills, and martial arts ability over traditional teaching methods. Li (2022), while exploring the impact of cooperative learning on improving the humanistic caring ability of nursing students in a virtual learning community environment, found that the observation group's satisfaction rate for all five items of teaching satisfaction was higher than that of the control group, and the differences were all statistically significant ($P<0.05$).

Chen (2022) pointed out that in cooperative learning, students can share high-quality learning resources, accelerate the improvement of comprehensive abilities, achieve a win-win effect for both learners, and export learning results well. Du Fang (2022) In college English teaching, adopting cooperative teaching methods is conducive to improving students' learning ability and teaching quality. Liu & You (2021) pointed out that the cooperative learning teaching model is a product of the new curriculum reform and has a significant effect on improving students' academic performance.

Related research shows that cooperative learning can generally improve students' academic performance, but from the perspective of the scope of research, mainly primary and secondary schools and English subjects are doing such research. For the traditional Chinese culture education in universities, it is a new attempt to apply cooperative learning methods to design courses and practical courses.

4. Cooperative learning and motivation

Men and Robinson (2018) conducted a questionnaire survey and interviews with non-English majors in military schools. The research found that cooperative learning can effectively improve the motivation for English learning, improve the evaluation of the English learning environment, and alleviate the degree of learning burnout. Li (2020) believes that the adoption of cooperative learning is of great significance, so that the dominant position of students can be fully reflected, and students can be masters of their own learning. Students have changed from passive learning in the past to active learning. Through cooperative learning, students have not only mastered knowledge and skills but also cultivated students' practical ability.

Liu (2020) believes that the application of the "cooperative learning method" is conducive to cultivating the learning interest and learning ability of middle school vocational students. Wang (2022) discovered after research that to maximize learning effectiveness, students need to establish the concept of active learning, give full play to their subjective activism in the learning process, and form an internal driving force for active learning. At the same time, they must handle the overall relationship of the learning team, understand the team members, enhance their enthusiasm for learning, create a good learning atmosphere, and provide external support for cooperative learning. Li (2021) believes that cooperative learning has effectively highlighted students' dominant position in teaching activities, enhanced students' awareness of active participation, and achieved remarkable results in teaching practice.

Liu (2022) discovered through analysis of the elements and effects of the classroom environment that cooperative learning has a certain scope of application and limitations in international Chinese classrooms and should be used rationally. For long-term classroom teaching, cooperative learning is appropriate and can increase the opportunities for students to practice Chinese and participate in learning. Ge (2022) believes that through cooperative learning, student's enthusiasm for learning can be fully mobilized and the effective cultivation of students' art literacy can be strengthened.

One of the principles of cooperative learning is assisting the other members of the group to understand the materials and achieve the shared goals. Every student in the cooperative learning method is responsible not only for his/her understanding but also for the understanding of the other members of the group. The mutual support among students facilitates the alleviation of demotivating factors such as shyness and insecurity, leading to an increase in motivation (Salamah, et al., 2024).

Studies conducted both domestically and internationally have indicated that cooperative learning can effectively enhance students' motivation. However, current research in China primarily focuses on the application of cooperative learning in basic education, with limited impact on teaching methods in colleges and universities. As teaching methods in Chinese higher education institutions continue to undergo reforms, it is inevitable that changes will occur. Exploring the implementation of cooperative learning in teaching Chinese traditional culture at the collegiate level can offer valuable insights for reforming classroom teaching methods in colleges and universities.

5. Cooperative learning and social skills

According to Gao and Zhao (2022), the distinguishing characteristic of the cooperative learning approach is its emphasis on transforming the learning culture and environment. Unlike traditional teaching methods that prioritize individual learning and competition, cooperative learning promotes mutual teaching and learning among students, fostering a cooperative atmosphere that enhances the learning process. A lot of studies have shown that the cooperative learning method can not only enhance students 'learning effect but also promote students' social development.

Liu (2020) believes that cooperative teaching method in the specific team cooperation process there will be different opinions, therefore, students should constantly communicate, constantly express their views, and refute others 'views, through this series will make students' communication ability and expression ability is improved, and let learners learn how to understand and listen to other ideas and opinions, learn how to respect and understand other students and know how to make decisions, how to moderate compromise, how to cooperate with others to solve problems, is conducive to students to develop a sense of cooperation.

Wang (2016) believes that the "cooperative learning method" is conducive to the solution of open questions. Students can cause the collision of student thinking and language communication when answering open questions and encourage students to have the courage to communicate. Buchenya (2021) believes that the application of the “cooperative learning method" is conducive to the cultivation of students' communication ability and strain ability. Zhang & Zhu (2022) found that students generally welcome and affirm cooperative learning; they more agreed with the conditions guarantee, group operation mode, cooperative learning tasks, achievement reporting and evaluation, and the role of teachers. Khan (2024) believes that the use of cooperative learning has shown teachers a commitment to fairness, social responsibility, and a concern for others. Now more than ever, our students need education that gives them the skills to understand and respect others as well as to be comfortable with differences.

The above research results of surface cooperative learning play a significant role in the following methods:

-Improvement of student's academic performance

-Improvement of student's learning motivation

-Students mastery of social skills

However, in the expression of the research results, it can also be seen that the research methods of cooperative learning in Chinese universities are not in-depth, and the application of cooperative learning is limited to primary and secondary education, which has something to do with the current education policies in China. Basic education took the lead in implementing the inquiry, cooperative, and interactive education reform with students as the main body, but with the continuous development of higher education, the curriculum reform of higher education must also be implemented. In the current study of cooperative learning, there are many methods and cases that can be applied to the reform of Chinese traditional culture curriculum in colleges and universities, the purpose of this study is to design a suitable university Chinese traditional culture course cooperative learning teaching mode, through the test of its effectiveness, build cooperative learning in the implementation of higher education in China.

2.5 Comparison of Traditional and Cooperative Learning Approach

2.5.1 Teaching Method

Traditional teaching methods are characterized by lecture-based instruction, in which the teacher is the primary source of knowledge and students are expected to listen, take notes, and memorize the information presented to them. This approach has been criticized for its passive and disengaging nature, which can limit students' ability to learn and retain information (Liu et al., 2023). In contrast, cooperative learning methods emphasize collaboration, active participation, and student-centered learning. In this approach, students work together in groups to solve problems, share their knowledge and skills, and actively engage with the material being taught (Johnson & Johnson, 1989).

Cooperative learning has been found to have a positive impact on students' learning outcomes and attitudes towards learning. A meta-analysis of 122 studies found that cooperative learning had a significant effect on academic achievement, with students in cooperative learning groups outperforming those in traditional classrooms (Johnson et al., 2014). Another study found that cooperative learning improved students' critical thinking skills and ability to apply knowledge in real-world situations (Stoddard & Grosskopf, 2018).

As a result, it could be stated that traditional teaching methods rely mainly on lecturing and rote memorization, while cooperative learning methods emphasize collaboration, active participation, and student-centered learning. Cooperative learning has been found to have a positive impact on students' learning outcomes and attitudes towards learning, making it a valuable alternative to traditional teaching methods.

TABLE 2.1 Comparison of Teaching Methods (Sources: Johnson et al., 2014; Stoddard & Grosskopf, 2018)

Aspect	Traditional Learning	Cooperative Learning
Teaching Method	Lecture-based, teacher-centered	Collaboration-focused, student-centered
Student Role	Passive information receivers	Active participants, knowledge sharers
Learning Approach	Memorization and repetition	Problem-solving, interactive learning
Learning Outcomes	Limited engagement, retention	Significant improvement in outcomes, engagement

Table 1 illustrates the main differences between traditional teaching methods and cooperative learning methods.

Research shows that cooperative learning positively impacts students' learning outcomes and attitudes. A meta-analysis of 122 studies found significant positive effects on Achievement Scores in cooperative learning settings (Johnson et al., 2014). Another study indicated improvements in critical thinking skills and real-world application of knowledge (Stoddard & Grosskopf, 2018)

2.5.2 Teaching Practice

In traditional teaching methods, the teacher is seen as the primary source of knowledge and authority in the classroom, and the focus is on maintaining classroom discipline. On the other hand, cooperative learning methods prioritize student autonomy and social interaction in the learning process. According to the Vygotskian theory of sociocultural learning, social interaction plays a critical role in cognitive development and learning (Vygotsky, 1978). In a cooperative learning environment, students can engage in meaningful discussions, ask questions, and receive feedback from their peers. This can lead to deeper learning and greater retention of knowledge (Johnson & Johnson, 1999).

Research has shown that cooperative learning methods can lead to improved academic achievement and social skills in students (Johnson & Johnson, 2009; Webb & Palincsar, 1996). By working collaboratively in groups, students develop communication skills, learn to work effectively with others, and gain a better understanding of different perspectives (Johnson & Johnson, 2009).Accordingly, while traditional teaching methods prioritize teachers' authority and classroom discipline, cooperative learning methods prioritize students' autonomy and social interaction, which can lead to improved academic achievement and social skills in students.

TABLE 2.2 Comparison of Teaching Practices (Sources: Johnson & Johnson, 2009; Webb & Palincsar, 1996)

Aspect	Traditional Learning	Cooperative Learning
Teacher's Role	Primary knowledge source, maintain discipline	Prioritize student autonomy, social interaction
Student Interaction	Limited interaction	High interaction through group work
Depth of Learning	Surface learning, memorization	Deep learning, knowledge internalization

Table 2 illustrates the main differences between traditional teaching practices and cooperative learning practices.

Research indicates that cooperative learning can lead to improved academic achievement and social skills (Johnson & Johnson, 2009; Webb & Palincsar, 1996).

Collaborative group work helps students develop communication skills, learn to work effectively with others, and understand different perspectives (Johnson & Johnson, 2009).

2.5.3 Teaching Materials

Traditional teaching methods in China rely heavily on the use of textbooks and other printed materials such as historical documents, poetry, and artworks to convey knowledge to students (Chen,2022). These materials are often seen as authoritative and are used to reinforce the teacher's lecture. The emphasis is on learning and memorizing the content of these materials through repetition and rote learning. This approach to teaching and learning is consistent with the Confucian tradition that emphasizes respect for authority and the importance of acquiring knowledge.

On the other hand, cooperative learning methods aim to engage students in active learning and promote collaboration among students. In this approach, a variety of teaching materials are used, including multimedia resources, group projects, and practical applications. The use of multimedia resources, such as videos and interactive simulations, can help to bring complex concepts to life and make them more accessible to students. Group projects and practical applications allow students to apply their knowledge to real-world problems and develop important skills such as communication, teamwork, and critical thinking

TABLE 2.3 Comparison of Teaching Materials (Source: Chen, 2022)

Aspect	Traditional Learning	Cooperative Learning
Teaching Materials	Primarily textbooks, historical documents	Multimedia resources, group projects, practical applications
Learning Approach	Repetition and memorization	Practical application, knowledge integration

Table 3 illustrates the main differences between traditional teaching materials and cooperative learning materials.

Traditional methods rely heavily on textbooks and other printed materials (Chen, 2022). Cooperative learning, however, employs a variety of materials, including multimedia resources, group projects, and practical applications to engage students actively.

2.5.4 Evaluation Method

Traditional teaching methods often rely on summative assessments such as exams, essays, and oral presentations, which focus on measuring students' knowledge and understanding of a particular subject. These types of assessments typically evaluate students' ability to recall and communicate information learned through lecture and memorization. In contrast, cooperative learning methods often use formative assessments such as group presentations, peer evaluations, and self-reflection activities, which focus on evaluating students' ability to apply the knowledge they have learned in the classroom to real-world situations. These types of assessments encourage active participation, critical thinking, and collaboration among students.

traditional teaching methods rely on summative assessments and lecture-based instruction, cooperative learning methods encourage active participation, collaboration, and formative assessments. These methods have been shown to improve academic performance, social skills, and motivation among students.

TABLE 2.4 Comparison of Evaluation Methods (Source: Chen, 2022)

Aspect	Traditional Learning	Cooperative Learning
Evaluation Methods	Summative assessments like exams, essays, and presentations	Formative assessments like group presentations, peer evaluations, and self-reflection
Evaluation Fcous	Measuring memory and understanding	Evaluating knowledge application and practical skills

Table 4 illustrates the main differences between traditional evaluation methods and cooperative learning evaluation methods.

Traditional methods focus on summative assessments (Chen, 2022), while cooperative learning methods emphasize formative assessments that encourage active participation, critical thinking, and collaboration.

According to the empirical research listed in this paper, the differences between traditional teaching methods and cooperative teaching methods are described as follows:

In terms of teaching methods, traditional teaching methods mainly rely on teaching and rote memorization, while cooperative learning methods emphasize collaboration, active participation and student-centered learning. In terms of teaching practice, traditional teaching methods emphasize teachers 'authority and classroom discipline, while cooperative learning methods emphasize students' autonomy and social interaction. In teaching materials, traditional teaching methods rely heavily on textbooks, historical documents, poetry, and artworks, while collaborative learning methods may combine a wider range of materials, such as multimedia resources, group projects, and practical applications. In terms of evaluation methods, traditional teaching methods are mainly written, oral and thesis, while cooperative learning may use more diverse methods, such as group presentation and peer evaluation.

TABLE 2.5 Summary diagram of the main differences between the traditional teaching method and the cooperative learning method

Aspect	Traditional Learning	Cooperative Learning
Teaching Method	Teacher-centered; lecture-based	Student-centered; group activities
Student Role	Passive receivers of information	Active participants; peer teaching
Interaction	Limited student interaction	High level of student interaction
Learning Environment	Competitive	Collaborative
Assessment	Individual-based; standardized tests	Group-based; performance assessments
Motivation	Extrinsic; grades and rewards	Intrinsic; peer support and group success
Skill Development	Focus on academic skills	Development of academic and social skills
Feedback	Primarily from the teacher	From peers and the teacher
Learning Pace	Uniform for all students	Differentiated; accommodates different paces
Focus	Memorization and individual performance	Understanding, collaboration, and application

2.6 Theoretical framework

The theoretical framework of this study encompasses various theories that underpin the concept and implementation of cooperative learning. These theories provide a comprehensive understanding of how cooperative learning influences student performance, motivation, and social skills.

1. Social Constructivism Theory

Social Constructivism Theory, primarily developed by Lev Vygotsky, posits that knowledge is constructed through social interactions and cultural contexts. According to Vygotsky, learning is a social process where students build knowledge through interactions with peers, teachers, and other individuals within their environment. Vygotsky introduced the concept of the Zone of Proximal Development (ZPD), which describes the range of tasks a learner can perform with guidance but not independently. Cooperative learning aligns with this theory as it involves students working together, enabling them to achieve higher levels of understanding through mutual support and collaboration (Vygotsky, 1978; Vygotsky, 1986). Constructivist learning theory emphasizes active engagement, where students are viewed as active participants in their learning journey, constructing knowledge through interactions and experiences (Campbell & Tran, 2023; Lenkauskaitė & Bubnys, 2020).

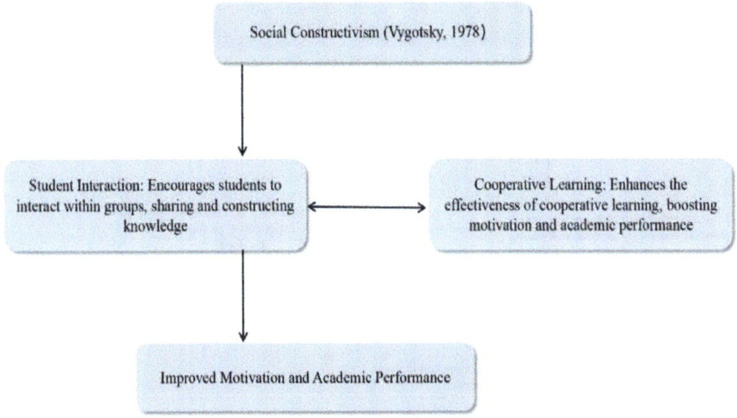

FIGURE 2.2: Supportive Role of Social Constructivism Theory

2. Humanistic Theory

Humanistic Theory, proposed by Carl Rogers, emphasizes the importance of personal growth and self-actualization in learning. This theory highlights the role of the learning environment in fostering a supportive and understanding atmosphere where students feel valued and respected. Cooperative learning embodies the principles of humanistic theory by creating a learning environment that promotes mutual respect, empathy, and personal development. It encourages students to express themselves freely, engage in meaningful interactions, and develop a sense of belonging and self-worth (Rogers, 1969).

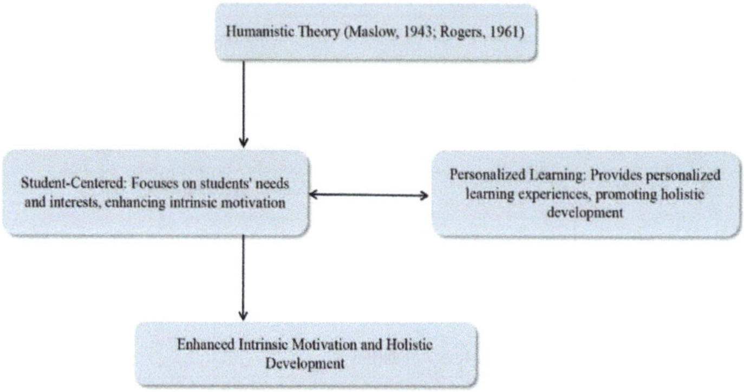

FIGURE 2.3: Supportive Role of Humanistic Theory

3. Group Dynamics Theory

John Dewey's concept of "democratic education" laid the foundation for Herbert Thelen's Group Dynamics Theory. Dewey emphasized the importance of democratic participation and critical thinking in education, advocating for active student engagement and collaborative decision-making (Dewey, 1916). Thelen expanded on this by focusing on the interactions within groups and their impact on individual learning and development. Group Dynamics Theory asserts that group interactions can enhance learning outcomes by promoting cooperation, communication, and mutual support among students. The theory identifies stages of group development, such as forming, storming, norming, and performing, which describe the evolving dynamics and roles within a group (Thelen, 1954; Tuckman, 1965, 1977). Kurt Lewin's work on group dynamics laid the foundation for understanding how individuals behave in group settings, focusing on aspects such as group processes, leadership, and group decision-making (Lewin,1947).Thelen also highlighted the importance of balancing task roles and maintenance roles to ensure group success and cohesion (Thelen, 1954).

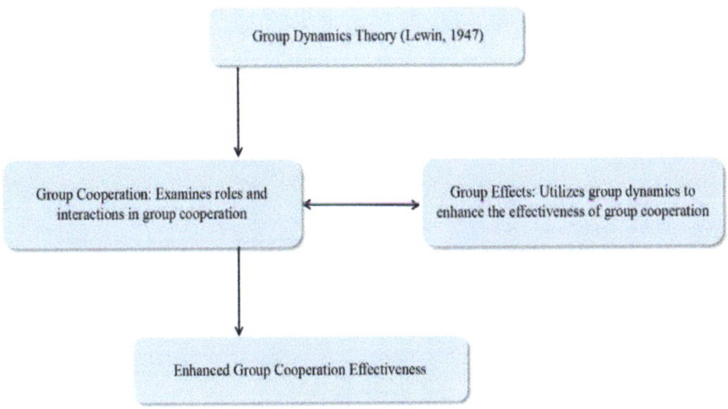

FIGURE 2.4: Supportive Role of Group Dynamics Theory

4. Social Interdependence Theory

The concept of social interdependence was initially proposed by Kurt Koffka and further developed by Kurt Lewin and Morton Deutsch. This theory posits that group members' interdependence significantly influences group dynamics and motivation. Positive interdependence occurs when group members perceive their success as linked to the success of their peers, fostering a collaborative environment. Conversely, negative interdependence arises when individuals see their success as dependent on others' failure. Cooperative learning leverages positive interdependence by creating shared goals and mutual support among students, leading to enhanced motivation, performance, and social skills (Johnson & Johnson, 2021).

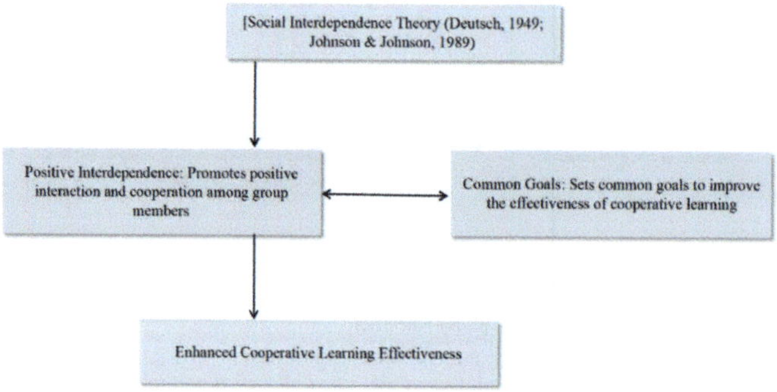

FIGURE 2.5: Supportive Role of Social Interdependence Theory

The theoretical framework for this study integrates multiple theories that collectively support the effectiveness of cooperative learning in enhancing academic performance, motivation, and social skills. By drawing on the principles of social constructivism, humanistic theory, group dynamics, social interdependence, cognitive development, learning motivation, and social skill development, this framework provides a comprehensive understanding of how cooperative learning can be optimally utilized to improve educational outcomes.

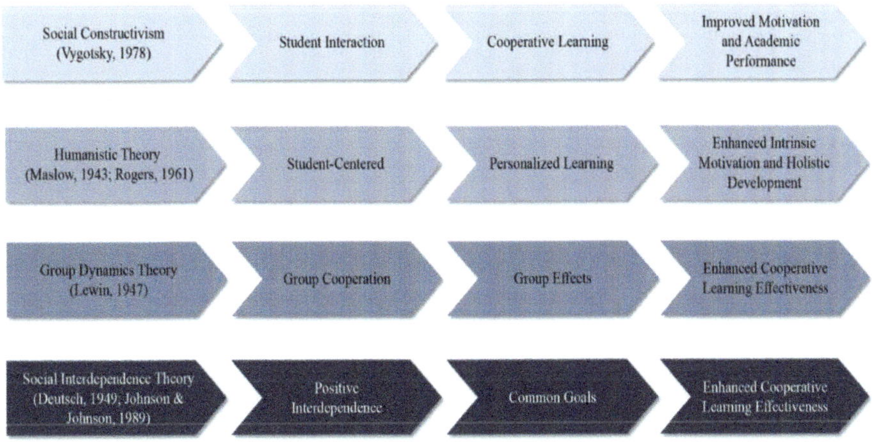

FIGURE 2.6: Theoretical Framework Graph

CHAPTER THREE

TRADITIONAL CHINESE CULTURE LESSON PLAN WITH COOPERATING LEARNING METHOD (TCC& CLM)

3.1 Introduction:

This chapter explores the critical process of teaching content selection, emphasizing the Analects as a cornerstone of traditional Chinese culture. Recognized as a classic, the Analects encapsulate Confucian values like benevolence, righteousness, and propriety, which have historically influenced various aspects of Chinese society and remain significant today (Wenhua, 2006). The chapter further discusses the design of teaching objectives and the implementation of cooperative learning models, such as the Student Team Achievement Divisions (STAD), to enhance student engagement and achievement (Slavin, 1983; Jamaludin & Mokhtar, 2018). It also addresses the comprehensive design of the teaching process and evaluation, emphasizing the importance of aligning educational content with intended learning outcomes through content validity assessments.

3.1.1 Teaching Content Selection

This study uses the Analects as the curriculum content of traditional Chinese culture, and in the final analysis, the Analects are an important core of traditional Chinese culture, and countless scholars are emphasizing this point.

In his book "New Interpretation of the Analects", Ma Yifu, a master of traditional Chinese studies, believes that the Analects are one of the classics of traditional Chinese culture, which epitomizes the core values of Confucianism, including benevolence, righteousness, propriety, wisdom, faith, and so on. These values profoundly influenced the political, economic, cultural, and ethical aspects of ancient China, and are still of great significance in modern society (Wenhua, 2006).

First, Yifu believes that the Analects emphasize the value of benevolence. In Confucianism, benevolence is regarded as the highest human moral quality. Benevolence is not only a moral requirement, but also a sign of personal cultivation and social harmony. Through the words and deeds of Confucius and his disciples, the Analects expound the connotation and practice of benevolence, providing people with a guide for moral behavior and interpersonal relationships.

Second, Yifu believes that the righteousness and propriety emphasized in the Analects are also the core values of Confucianism. Righteousness emphasizes moral justice, fairness, and honesty, while propriety emphasizes norms and rituals in social life. Through the elaboration of these two concepts, Confucius conveyed a kind of idea of "governing the country and leveling the world", believing that politicians should govern the country with virtue and act with courtesy, so that society can achieve a harmonious and stable state.

In addition, the concepts of wisdom and faith in the Analects are also very important. Wisdom represents the ability to know, think, judge, etc., while faith represents honesty and reliability in relationships. The emphasis on these two concepts provides an important theoretical basis for education and talent selection in ancient

China, and also plays an important role in enlightenment and guidance in modern society.

The famous scholar Qian Mu also mentioned the important position of the Analects in traditional Chinese culture in his book "Outline of National History" (Qian, 1996). He believes that the Analects, as one of the most important classics in traditional Chinese culture, have extremely profound historical and cultural significance. The Confucian ideology embodied in the Analects, including core values such as benevolence, righteousness, propriety, wisdom, and faith, constitutes an important part of traditional Chinese culture and has had a profound impact on Chinese society and culture (Qian, 1996).

The Analects of thought embodies the core values of traditional Chinese culture, of which "benevolence" is the most important. The "benevolence" mentioned in the Analects includes both the love and concern of the individual for others, as well as the concern and concern for society and mankind. This kind of "benevolence" influence the thinking and behavior of Chinese, making them pay attention to their inner cultivation and moral behavior, but also pay attention to the overall interests of society and mankind. The Analects also emphasize the concept of "etiquette", which is a very important concept in traditional Chinese culture, which reflects not only the importance that Chinese attach to etiquette, but also to the relationship between the individual and society.

By studying the Analects, people can better understand the core values of traditional Chinese culture and draw inspiration and guidance from them. At the same time, the Analects also provide a way for people to better understand Chinese history and reality. Throughout the long years of Chinese history, Confucianism has been dominant, and the content of ideas in the Analects has influenced countless historical events and figures. For example, Confucius's idea of "benevolent government" in the Analects became a basic paradigm for governing the country in ancient China. At the same time, the Analects also profoundly influenced Chinese's ideas and behaviors, and this influence continues to this day.

According to educator Ye Jiaying, the Analects is one of the cores of traditional Chinese culture, and it has had a profound impact on Chinese's ideas and behaviors (Ye, 1996). In her book "Analects of Confucius", Ye Jiaying conducted an in-depth discussion and analysis of the value and significance of the Analects, as well as its enlightenment and guiding role in modern society.

The Analects holds a significant position as a classic work on Confucianism, showcasing the utmost importance of its teachings. Confucianism places great emphasis on human moral character and relationships, and the Analects serve as a pinnacle of Confucian thought. Within its pages lie the fundamental values of Confucianism, including benevolence, righteousness, propriety, wisdom, and faith, which form the essence of traditional Chinese culture. Through shaping behaviour, speech, and thought, the Analects reveal the true meaning and spirit of Confucianism.

Moreover, the Analects have had a profound impact on the ideas and behaviours of the Chinese people. Throughout the extensive timeline of Chinese history, Confucianism has stood as a prominent ideology, with the Analects representing one of its greatest masterpieces. Across various eras, the continuous study and exploration of the Analects have played a vital role in fostering the development of traditional Chinese culture. Furthermore, they have left an indelible mark on shaping the ideological concepts and behavioural patterns of the Chinese populace.

Chaoming is a famous Chinese philosopher and scholar, and in his book The Wisdom of the Analects, he expounded the important position and significance of the Analects in traditional Chinese culture (Yang, 2016) 。Chaoming pointed out that the Analects is a treasure of Chinese culture, which is not only an important part of traditional Chinese culture, but also one of the important sources of Chinese ideas and values. In the Analects, we can see the core values of Confucianism, such as benevolence, righteousness, propriety, wisdom, faith, etc., which are considered the most important parts of Chinese culture (Yang, 2016).

Chaoming emphasized that by studying the Analects, people can better understand the connotation and essence of traditional Chinese culture. The wisdom and values in the Analects can help us understand the basic ideas of Chinese culture about human survival and development, and then help us better face the challenges and problems of modern society.

At the same time, Yang Chaoming believes that the ideas and values embodied in the Analects are of universal significance. These values do not apply only to traditional Chinese culture, but can have an impact and enlightenment on a global scale. Therefore, by studying the Analects, we can not only better understand and carry forward traditional Chinese culture, but also help us better understand the development and progress of human civilization.

In short, Yang Chaoming emphasized the importance and significance of the Analects in traditional Chinese culture in his writings. Studying the Analects can not only help us better understand the connotation and essence of traditional Chinese culture, but also help us better cope with the challenges and problems of modern society. At the same time, through studying the Analects, we can also find that the wisdom and values contained in it have universal significance and have an important enlightenment effect on the development of global human civilization.

To sum up, as an important part of traditional Chinese culture, the Analects have extremely important value and significance. Through the study and study of the Analects, we can better understand and comprehend the connotation and essence of traditional Chinese culture. At the same time, through studying the Analects, we can also find that the wisdom and values contained in it have universal significance and have an important enlightenment effect on the development of global human civilization.

3.2 Curriculum Design

3.2.1 Teaching objectives design

The teaching objectives guide and guide the entire specific teaching activities, and without the teaching objectives, the teaching activities will become purposeless. The teaching goal is for the teacher to have a standard and purpose for class, and it is also conducive to teachers to find suitable teaching methods, and it is also a standard for evaluating teachers and assessing whether students have completed teaching goals.

Vocational colleges and universities should not only plan their cultivation objectives according to the employment direction of students and the needs of the society, but also cultivate senior talents with good professional ethics and ideological standards, so it is also a top priority to strengthen vocational college and university students' knowledge of traditional Chinese culture and use traditional Chinese culture to enrich their professional ethics and ideological awareness.

This paper hopes to cultivate students' core literacy, social skills and learning motivation through the teaching method of "cooperative learning method", combined with the syllabus of "Chinese Traditional Culture", the teaching objectives of this paper mainly select two chapters in the Analects as teaching examples, and the teaching objectives mainly include knowledge and skill objectives, process and method goals, emotional attitudes and values, and core literacy cultivation goals.

-Knowledge and Skills Objectives:

Students will gain an in-depth understanding of the themes and ideas of the Analects, including the concepts of benevolence, propriety, and filial piety.

Students will be able to analyse and interpret Confucian texts and demonstrate the ability to apply these ideas to contemporary issues and challenges.

Students will develop strong critical thinking and analytical skills by reading texts and related materials.

- Process and method objectives:

Students will engage in active, collaborative learning, including group discussions, co-writing, and cyclical brainstorming.

Students will learn to interact with text through a variety of mediums, including writing, speaking, and presentation.

Students will be exposed to a variety of teaching methods, including lectures, readings, and multimedia resources.

- Emotional attitudes and values:

Students will develop an appreciation of moral and ethical principles inherent in Confucian teachings, such as respect for authority, the importance of self-improvement, and the cultivation of virtues.

Students will develop the ability to self-reflect and reflect, learning to apply Confucian teachings to their own lives and values.

Students will learn how to develop emotional intelligence and develop positive emotional attitudes towards learning and relationships.

-Core Literacy Training Objectives:

Students will develop key skills and traits that are critical to personal and professional success, such as self-discipline, perseverance, and responsibility.

Students will develop a sense of social responsibility and civic engagement and learn to apply Confucian teachings to their roles as responsible citizens.

Students will gain a deeper understanding of the importance of lifelong learning and self-improvement and learn to apply Confucian teachings to personal and professional development.

3.2.2 Discussion on the teaching mode of Chinese traditional culture in vocational colleges and universities based on cooperative learning

1. Student Team Achievement Divisions (STAD)

The STAD model, proposed by American educational psychologist Robert Slavin in 1983 (Slavin,1983), is a cooperative learning model in which students work as a team to achieve academic goals. The STAD model is designed to promote academic achievement, positive interdependence, personal responsibility, and social skills development (Jamaludin, & Mokhtar, 2018).

A typical STAD model involves several steps:

- Students are divided into groups of four to six, with each group member having a different level of competence in the subjects taught.

- The teacher first lectures on a lesson or a teaching unit and then takes a quiz or quiz to assess the student's understanding of the material.

- It is the responsibility of each team member to learn and understand the material.

- At the end of the individual study time, team members work together to ensure that each member has a good understanding of the material.

- The teacher then evaluates the team's performance, which will assess their mastery of key ideas through presentations, quizzes and apps.

- The teams with the highest scores are recognized and rewarded, individual scores are also recorded, and their progress will be measured by accumulated points.

In fact, STAD is based on the realization of pedagogical teaching methods (Felder & Bren, 2001; Ghaith, 2001). Studies have shown that STAD models are effective in improving not only academics, but also social skills and attitudes towards school.

However, in the teaching process of traditional Chinese culture courses, STAD does not fully adapt. According to the characteristics of Chinese traditional culture courses and vocational university students, combined with STAD, a teaching model that conforms to the cooperative learning method in Chinese traditional culture courses is designed, and the basic model is as follows:

- Interactive warm-ups: Teachers can start the class with interactive warm-up activities that engage students and set the tone for the lesson. For example, teachers can ask students to share their favourite texts or ask them to identify traditional Chinese cultural symbols.

- Explanation and class presentation: The teacher gives a brief explanation and statement of the topic, including the interpretation of the original text, the meaning of the words, and the historical background of the time. In this session, teachers can also combine various teaching materials such as videos, music, and literary works to engage students and deepen their understanding of traditional Chinese culture.

- Team learning: At the end of the presentation, students are divided into groups of 3 to 4, each team member with a different level of competence in the subjects taught. Start using puzzle puzzles, peer tutoring, etc. in cooperative learning to organize students for group learning. Take the puzzle method, for example: the teacher assigns each team member a specific task, such as reading a specific part of the text, summarizing important information, or identifying key concepts. Each student is then given time to complete their tasks independently.

- Theme sharing: At the end of the individual study time, team members work together to ensure that each member has a good understanding of the material. Team members share their findings and present the topic as a group discussion. Presentations can take the form of speeches, articles, or other formats, during which the teacher can walk around the class to provide support and guidance.

-Classroom evaluation: At the end of the team learning session, teachers conduct individual and group assessments, the team with the highest score is recognized and rewarded, and the individual score is recorded.

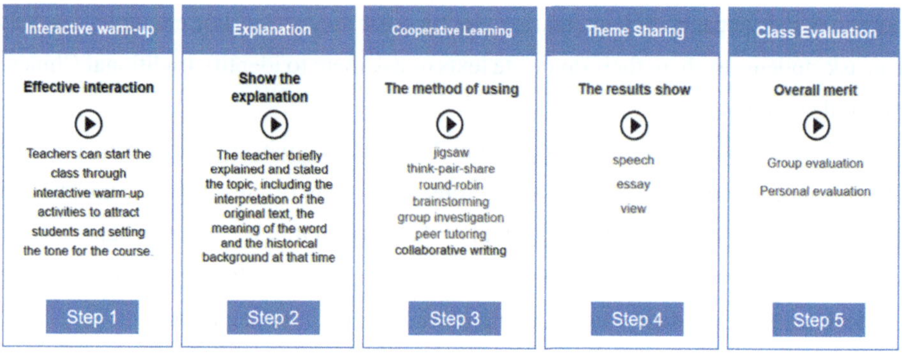

FIGURE 3.1: The Teaching Process

2. Interactive pedagogy

The main purpose of the cooperative learning method in this study is to enhance the understanding of excellent traditional Chinese culture, help students learn to learn, and cultivate students' independent learning ability, communication and expression ability. Therefore, when carrying out teaching design, we should pay attention to the cultivation of students' abilities in these aspects, and teachers need to carefully design the teaching process and adopt "interactive teaching" in the teaching process The form can fully stimulate students' interest in learning, take interesting situational interaction can attract students' attention to the classroom, adopt the form of problem-guided interaction can allow students to learn knowledge points in a step-by-step manner, to achieve orderly learning from easy to difficult, and not easy to make students tired, through continuous problem solving can stimulate students' curiosity and interest in learning.

The theory of interactive teaching (Turgunova & Abdurahimovna, 2023), initially introduced by Palincsar at Michigan State University in 1982, has undergone subsequent research and development. This theory builds upon the scaffold teaching theory as its foundation. Interactive teaching is characterized by its focus on nurturing students through specific strategies aimed at promoting understanding. In interactive classrooms, there is a strong emphasis on mutual support and facilitation among learners, enabling both students and teachers to grasp the teaching objectives. This approach encourages students to respond more actively and constructively, fostering a dynamic and engaging learning environment. Looking at the concept of interactive classroom teaching, as far as teachers are concerned, teachers guide students to communicate and cooperate with each other in different interactive forms, create an active interactive atmosphere, and enhance students' enthusiasm for participating in teaching activities. As far as students are concerned, interactive classrooms fully reflect the main position of students in learning, and students can build a platform to show themselves, and obtain innovative opportunities for mutual assistance and cooperation, independent inquiry.

Interactive teaching has the following features:

Student-centred learning: Interactive teaching focuses on the student, not the teacher. Teachers act as facilitators, guiding students through the learning process and providing support when needed.

-Active learning: Interactive teaching emphasizes the active participation of students, and involves students in various activities, such as discussion, debate, and problem-solving exercises.

- Collaborative Learning: Interactive teaching encourages students to work together in small groups or in pairs, share ideas and knowledge, and support each other in learning.

- Feedback: Interactive teaching provides students with frequent feedback from teachers and peers. This feedback helps students understand their strengths and weaknesses and adjust their learning strategies as needed.

- Technology integration: Interactive teaching often utilizes technology to facilitate learning, such as online discussion forums, interactive whiteboards, and multimedia resources.

To apply the theory of interactive teaching to the teaching of Chinese traditional culture in vocational colleges, there are the following aspects:

- Group Discussions: Students are encouraged to participate in group discussions to explore and analyse traditional Chinese cultural concepts and values. This will help students deepen their understanding of the material and gain insights from their peers.

- Role play: Through role play, students understand traditional Chinese cultural customs and beliefs, such as the concept of filial piety or the importance of respecting the old and loving the young.

- Case Studies: Students are presented with case studies that explore real-world. examples of traditional Chinese culture, such as the role of Confucianism in Chinese society. This will help students connect theoretical concepts with practical applications.

- Interactive Lectures: Use interactive lectures that combine activities and discussions to engage students and encourage active learning. For example, use multimedia resources to illustrate traditional Chinese cultural practices or explore the historical context in which they developed.

- Group projects: Students are encouraged to work in groups to explore and analyze traditional Chinese cultural customs and values. This will help them develop teamwork and collaboration skills while deepening their understanding of the material.

By combining the cooperative learning method with the specific characteristics of vocational university students, the author devised a teaching mode that aligns with both cooperative learning and interactive learning principles for the Chinese traditional culture course in vocational universities. The teaching mode is visually represented in the figure below:

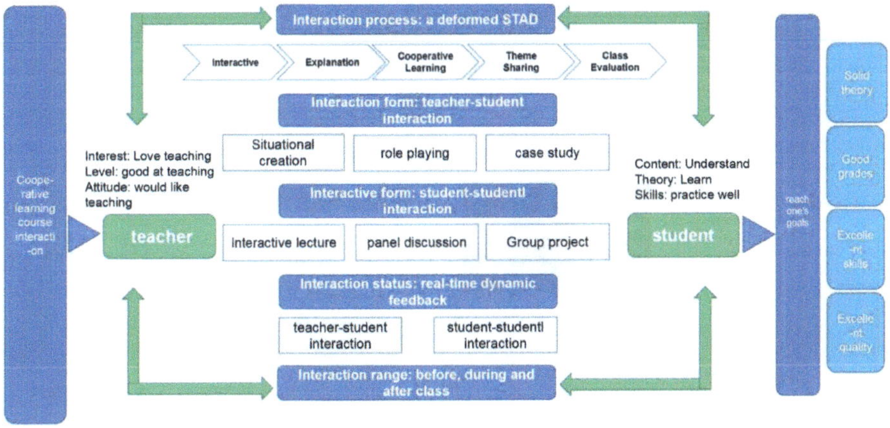

FIGURE 3.2: Illustration of the teaching process

3.2.3 Teaching process design

Cooperative learning is an effective teaching method that promotes student participation, motivation and enthusiasm, and encourages students to work together in small groups to achieve common goals. Designing a cooperative learning process that maximizes student learning and makes it easy to implement focuses on three phases: before class, in class , and after class.

Before class:

Prior to the start of the class, students engage in independent inquiry activities, including reading and absorbing relevant materials, such as watching a documentary film on China's classical works, to develop a foundational understanding of traditional Chinese culture. They also undertake task inquiries by previewing the original text of the Analects of Confucius, contemplating its applicability in today's society. Additionally, students conduct study situation research, where they participate in qualitative research and discussions based on their individual circumstances.

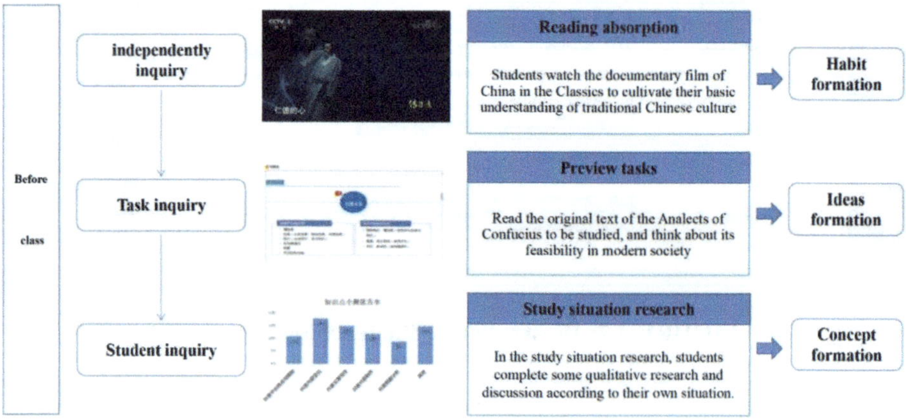

FIGURE 3.3: Illustration of work before class

In class:

During the class, interactive activities are employed to facilitate learning. Students are encouraged to read the text and identify key themes and concepts, fostering critical thinking. They are also prompted to ask questions and share areas of interest for class discussion, promoting engagement and deeper understanding. The instructor provides explanations of the original interpretation, ensuring clarity and comprehension. Additionally, the application steps and implementation of the cooperative learning method are explained, emphasizing its benefits in collaborative learning. Cooperative learning techniques such as Jigsaw, think-pair-share, round-robin brainstorming, group investigation, and peer tutoring are utilized to enhance active participation and knowledge sharing among students. Theme sharing sessions provide opportunities for students to showcase their findings through speeches, essays, and personal viewpoints, further enhancing their communication skills. Finally, class evaluation is conducted to assess the overall merit of the learning experience, comprising both group evaluations and personal evaluations to provide comprehensive feedback.

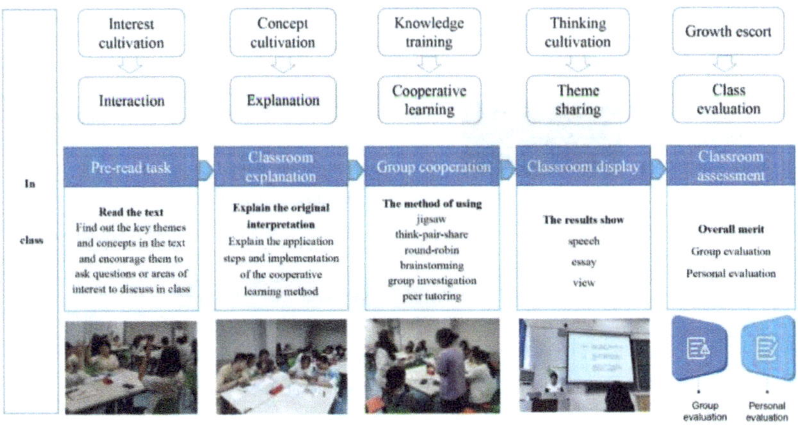

FIGURE 3.4: Illustration of work in class

After class:

During the class, various activities take place to foster interaction and facilitate learning. Students are encouraged to actively engage with the text by identifying key themes and concepts, while also raising questions or areas of interest for class discussion. The instructor provides explanations of the original interpretation, including the steps and implementation of the cooperative learning method. Cooperative learning methods such as Jigsaw, think-pair-share, round-robin brainstorming, group investigation, and peer tutoring are utilized to enhance collaborative learning experiences. Theme sharing is conducted to showcase the outcomes, which can be presented through speeches, essays, or personal viewpoints. Finally, class evaluation encompasses both group evaluations and individual evaluations to assess the overall merits of the learning process.

Figure 3.5: Illustration of work after class below the figure.

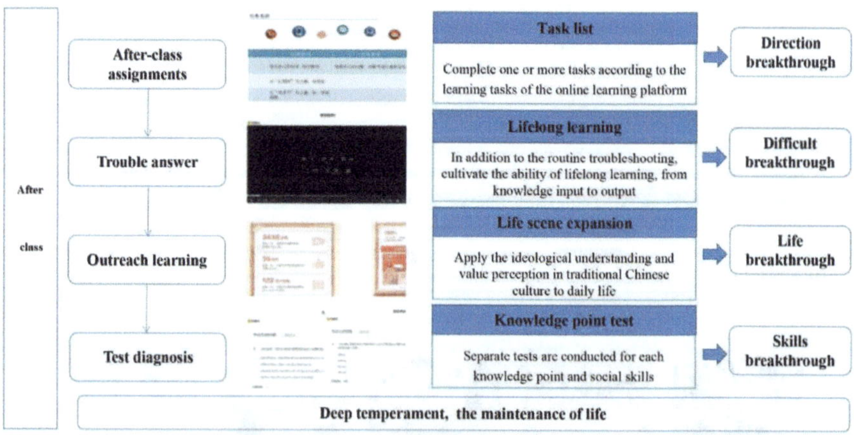

3.2.4 Teaching evaluation design

Teaching evaluation is a multi-faceted and multi-dimensional evaluation, the main evaluation includes teaching process and teaching results, etc., teaching evaluation is mainly to evaluate the teaching work of teachers and the learning effectiveness of students. For teachers' teaching work, watch checklists are used to assess teachers' implementation of cooperative learning methods, including whether they effectively organize group activities and provide guidance and feedback. Use student surveys to gather feedback on teachers' effectiveness in facilitating group discussions and developing critical thinking skills. Analyse student performance data to determine if there is a correlation between teachers' teaching work and student learning outcomes.

For student outcomes, formative assessments are used to assess student learning throughout the course, including quizzes, individual assignments, and group projects. Final exams are held to assess students' mastery of the Analects in traditional Chinese culture and their ability to apply Confucian principles to contemporary issues. Use student surveys to gather feedback on the effectiveness of cooperative learning methods in promoting student engagement, teamwork, and critical thinking skills.

In general, the teaching evaluation of traditional Chinese culture courses based on cooperative learning should be designed as a comprehensive evaluation of teachers' teaching work and students' learning outcomes. This can be achieved by combining formative and summative assessments, watch lists, student surveys, and student performance data analysis. By evaluating both areas, teachers can identify areas for improvement and adjust their teaching strategies to better meet the needs of students.

3.2.5 Teaching content selection

This study uses the Analects as the curriculum content of traditional Chinese culture, and in the final analysis, the Analects are an important core of traditional Chinese culture, and countless scholars are emphasizing this point.

In his book "New Interpretation of the Analects", Ma Yifu, a master of traditional Chinese studies, believes that the Analects are one of the classics of traditional Chinese culture, which epitomizes the core values of Confucianism, including benevolence, righteousness, propriety, wisdom, faith, and so on. These values profoundly influenced the political, economic, cultural, and ethical aspects of ancient China, and are still of great significance in modern society (Wenhua, 2006).

First, Yifu believes that the Analects emphasize the value of benevolence. In Confucianism, benevolence is regarded as the highest human moral quality. Benevolence is not only a moral requirement, but also a sign of personal cultivation and social harmony. Through the words and deeds of Confucius and his disciples, the Analects expound the connotation and practice of benevolence, providing people with a guide for moral behavior and interpersonal relationships.

Second, Yifu believes that the righteousness and propriety emphasized in the Analects are also the core values of Confucianism. Righteousness emphasizes moral justice, fairness, and honesty, while propriety emphasizes norms and rituals in social life. Through the elaboration of these two concepts, Confucius conveyed a kind of idea of "governing the country and leveling the world", believing that politicians should govern the country with virtue and act with courtesy, so that society can achieve a harmonious and stable state.

In addition, the concepts of wisdom and faith in the Analects are also very important. Wisdom represents the ability to know, think, judge, etc., while faith represents honesty and reliability in relationships. The emphasis on these two concepts provides an important theoretical basis for education and talent selection in ancient China, and also plays an important role in enlightenment and guidance in modern society.

The famous scholar Qian Mu also mentioned the important position of the Analects in traditional Chinese culture in his book "Outline of National History" (Qian, 1996). He believes that the Analects, as one of the most important classics in traditional Chinese culture, have extremely profound historical and cultural significance. The Confucian ideology embodied in the Analects, including core values such as benevolence, righteousness, propriety, wisdom, and faith, constitutes an important part of traditional Chinese culture and has had a profound impact on Chinese society and culture (Qian, 1996).

The Analects of thought embodies the core values of traditional Chinese culture, of which "benevolence" is the most important. The "benevolence" mentioned in the Analects includes both the love and concern of the individual for others, as well as the concern and concern for society and mankind. This kind of "benevolence" influence the thinking and behavior of Chinese, making them pay attention to their inner cultivation and moral behavior, but also pay attention to the overall interests of society and mankind. The Analects also emphasize the concept of "etiquette", which is a very important concept in traditional Chinese culture, which reflects not only the importance that Chinese attach to etiquette, but also to the relationship between the individual and society.

By studying the Analects, people can better understand the core values of traditional Chinese culture and draw inspiration and guidance from them. At the same time, the Analects also provide a way for people to better understand Chinese history and reality. Throughout the long years of Chinese history, Confucianism has been dominant, and the content of ideas in the Analects has influenced countless historical events and figures. For example, Confucius's idea of "benevolent government" in the Analects became a basic paradigm for governing the country in ancient China. At the same time, the Analects also profoundly influenced Chinese's ideas and behaviors, and this influence continues to this day.

According to educator Ye Jiaying, the Analects is one of the cores of traditional Chinese culture, and it has had a profound impact on Chinese's ideas and behaviors (Ye, 1996). In her book "Analects of Confucius", Ye Jiaying conducted an in-depth discussion and analysis of the value and significance of the Analects, as well as its enlightenment and guiding role in modern society.

The Analects holds a significant position as a classic work on Confucianism, showcasing the utmost importance of its teachings. Confucianism places great emphasis on human moral character and relationships, and the Analects serve as a pinnacle of Confucian thought. Within its pages lie the fundamental values of Confucianism, including benevolence, righteousness, propriety, wisdom, and faith, which form the essence of traditional Chinese culture. Through shaping behavior, speech, and thought, the Analects reveal the true meaning and spirit of Confucianism.

Moreover, the Analects have had a profound impact on the ideas and behaviors of the Chinese people. Throughout the extensive timeline of Chinese history, Confucianism has stood as a prominent ideology, with the Analects representing one of its greatest masterpieces. Across various eras, the continuous study and exploration of the Analects have played a vital role in fostering the development of traditional Chinese culture. Furthermore, they have left an indelible mark on shaping the ideological concepts and behavioral patterns of the Chinese populace.

Chaoming is a famous Chinese philosopher and scholar, and in his book The Wisdom of the Analects, he expounded the important position and significance of the Analects in traditional Chinese culture (Yang, 2016) 。Chaoming pointed out that the Analects is a treasure of Chinese culture, which is not only an important part of traditional Chinese culture, but also one of the important sources of Chinese ideas and values. In the Analects, we can see the core values of Confucianism, such as benevolence, righteousness, propriety, wisdom, faith, etc., which are considered the most important parts of Chinese culture (Yang, 2016).

Chaoming emphasized that by studying the Analects, people can better understand the connotation and essence of traditional Chinese culture. The wisdom and values in the Analects can help us understand the basic ideas of Chinese culture about human survival and development, and then help us better face the challenges and problems of modern society.

At the same time, Yang Chaoming believes that the ideas and values embodied in the Analects are of universal significance. These values do not apply only to traditional Chinese culture, but can have an impact and enlightenment on a global scale. Therefore, by studying the Analects, we can not only better understand and carry forward traditional Chinese culture, but also help us better understand the development and progress of human civilization.

In short, Yang Chaoming emphasized the importance and significance of the Analects in traditional Chinese culture in his writings. Studying the Analects can not only help us better understand the connotation and essence of traditional Chinese culture, but also help us better cope with the challenges and problems of modern society. At the same time, through studying the Analects, we can also find that the wisdom and values contained in it have universal significance and have an important enlightenment effect on the development of global human civilization.

To sum up, as an important part of traditional Chinese culture, the Analects have extremely important value and significance. Through the study and study of the Analects, we can better understand and comprehend the connotation and essence of traditional Chinese culture, and at the same time, through studying the Analects, we can also find that the wisdom and values contained in it have universal significance and have an important enlightenment effect on the development of global human civilization.

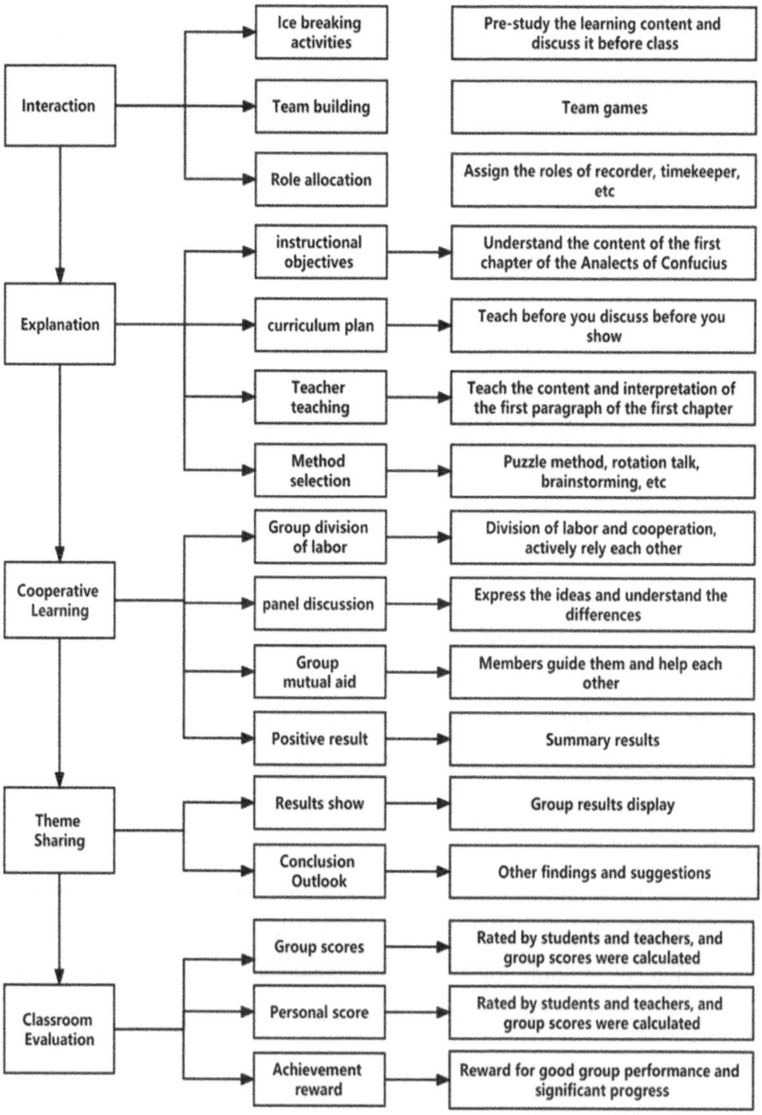

FIGURE 3.6: Table of Course steps

3.2.6 Content validity of the prototype module

Content validity evaluation is a crucial and intricate step in the tool development process, particularly when measuring complex constructs in social and administrative pharmacy research. This study conducted a content validity evaluation of a developed prototype module to ensure it effectively reflects the intended educational content.

Xu Aiai et al. (2021) suggest that content validity can be assessed using four methods: expert judgment, statistical analysis, retest analysis, and empirical evaluation. Among these, expert judgment is widely used for educational modules. Lynn (1986) emphasized that involving at least five experts can enhance the reliability and representativeness of the results.

In this study, feedback from subject matter experts and experienced educators was used to identify potential issues and make necessary revisions. Five content experts provided ratings and feedback on the module's content.

To systematically evaluate the content validity of the module, the researchers designed an assessment form based on the methods of Almanasreh & Chen (2019), detailed in Appendix V, with a simplified example shown in Table 1. Each part of the module was rated by three content experts on a scale from 1 (strongly disagree) to 5 (strongly agree). Additionally, these experts provided valuable comments and suggestions, which helped improve the module's content.

Through this rigorous evaluation process, the researchers ensured the scientific accuracy and reliability of the module content, laying a solid foundation for its application in educational practice.

3.3 Curriculum Sessions

3.3.1 Session ONE: Understanding the Analects of Confucius

<table>
<tr><td></td><td></td><td></td><td>Date</td><td></td><td></td></tr>
<tr><td colspan="2"></td><td colspan="4"></td></tr>
<tr><td colspan="2"></td><td colspan="4">

- Knowledge of the Four Books and Five Classics
- Basic understanding of the Analects of Confucius and its significance in Chinese culture
- Be able to identify and analyse key themes and concepts in the Analects of Confucius
- Develop a basic knowledge of Confucius and an understanding of his philosophy and its relevance to modern society

</td></tr>
<tr><td colspan="2"></td><td colspan="4"></td></tr>
<tr><td colspan="2"></td><td colspan="4"></td></tr>
<tr><td colspan="2"></td><td colspan="4"></td></tr>
</table>

of Zhou Gongdan, the younger brother of King Wu of Zhou, was first ruled by Bo Dou, the son of Zhou Gongdan. Among the many states in the Zhou Dynasty, Lu was the 'Zongbang' of the Ji family name and the 'Wangguo' of the vassals, so 'the closest thing Zhou rituals, and the world said, 'The Zhou rituals are all in Lu.'

**B
e
f
o
r
e**

A

B
.

	2 . a .

3.3.2 Session TWO: Analects of Philology, Part 1

			Date		
		1.1 Confucius said, "Learn something and then review and practice it frequently. Isn't it a pleasure? Have friends coming from afar. Isn't it a joy? Not being well understood, but I neither complain nor get angry. Isn't it a gentleman bearing?"			

	A . B . D . 2 . a .

3.3.3 Session THREE: Analects of Philology, No. 1

			Date		
		1.4 Zeng Zi said, "Everyday I examine myself many times. Do I do my best when doing things for others? Am I honest and reliable when associating with friends? Whether do I review and practise what my teachers teach me?			

	A B D 2 a

3.3.4 Session FOUR: Analects of Philology, PART 1

<table>
<tr><td></td><td></td><td></td><td>Date</td><td></td><td></td></tr>
<tr><td colspan="2"></td><td colspan="4"></td></tr>
<tr><td colspan="2"></td><td colspan="4"></td></tr>
<tr><td colspan="2"></td><td colspan="4">1.6 Confucius said, "Together with your parents, you should show filial devotion and obedience to them; while out of home, you should obey your teachers. Words and deeds should be cautious. Keep honest and reliable and taciturn. Show universal love to the broad masses and be close to the noble-minded persons. If still having some leeway after earnestly practising what you advocate above, you should study historical documents and try to learn more knowledge."</td></tr>
<tr><td colspan="2"></td><td colspan="4"></td></tr>
<tr><td colspan="2"></td><td colspan="4">HYPERLINK
"https://baike.baidu.com/item/%E8%87%AA%E7%84%B6%E7%A7%91%E5%AD%A6/2
6
0
5
3</td></tr>
</table>

	A B D 2 a

3.3.5 Session FIVE: Analects of Philology PART 2

			Date		
		PART 2			
		1.14 Confucius said, "Gentlemen seek neither sufficient food nor comfortable lives, but they are nimble in action and cautions in words and go to noble-minded people so as to perfect themselves day by day. If they do like this, then they can be thought perfect in learning."			

	A B D 2 a

3.3.6 Session SIX: The Analects are the second part of the political chapter

<table>
<tr><td></td><td></td><td></td><td>Date</td><td></td><td></td></tr>
<tr><td colspan="2"></td><td colspan="4"></td></tr>
<tr><td colspan="2"></td><td colspan="4"></td></tr>
<tr><td colspan="2"></td><td colspan="4">2.10 Confucius said, “If you want to know a person, you should analyze the motives of his words and deeds, observe the way he takes and examine what he is up to with ease of mind. If so, how can a person cover up himself? How can a person cover up himself?”</td></tr>
<tr><td colspan="2"></td><td colspan="4"></td></tr>
<tr><td colspan="2"></td><td colspan="4"></td></tr>
</table>

	A B D 2 a

3.3.7 Session SEVEN: Analects are the second part of the political chapter

			Date		
		2.17 Confucius said, “You, do you understand what I have taught you? If you do, say yes; otherwise, just say no. This is wisdom.”			

	A B D 2 a

3.3.8 Session EIGHT: Analects are the second in politics

			Date		
	2.15 Confucius said, “Only study but not think, you’ll be perplexed without any gains; only indulge in idle dreams but not study, you’ll suffer from misgivings and hesitate all the time.”				

	A B D 2 a

3.3.9 Session NINE: Analects of the Eight, Part III

			Date		

	3.15 Whenever entering the temple of the lord's ancestors, Confucius would ask questions about everything. Someone said, "Who says that this person knows proprieties? Whenever he enters the temple of the lord's ancestors, he consults others about everything." Learning this, Confucius said, "This is in itself a sort of propriety."
	A

	D 2 a

3.3.10 Session TEN: Analects of the Eight, Part III

			Date		

	3.19 Duke Ding of Lu (i.e. the lord of the country Lu) asked, "How does a lord order his courtiers and how do the courtiers serve their lord?" Confucius said, "A lord gives orders to his courtiers according to the proprieties while the courtiers serve their lord with loyalty."
	A B D 2 a

3.3.11 Session ELEVEN: The Analects of Ren Fourth

			Date		
	4.5 Confucius said, "Riches and honors are something everyone wants. But, if they are improperly obtained, then we should not enjoy them. Poorness and humbleness are something everyone detests. But if they are improperly eliminated, then we'd rather not free ourselves from them. If gentlemen lack humanity and virtue, how can they be considered gentlemen? Gentlemen don't depart from humanity and virtue just in a short period of time of a dinner. Even at the most critical moment, gentlemen must act according to the principle of humanity and virtue. And even destitute and homeless, they can act according to the principle of humanity and virtue."				

	A B D 2 a

3.3.12 Session TWELVE: Analects of Ren Fourth

			Date		
	4.14 Confucius said, “Don’t be afraid that you have no official posts. What you should be afraid of is not having learnt something which can help you keep a foothold.”				
	this teaching: "Do not suffer from positionlessness, suffer from standing; do not suffer from self-knowledge, seek to know also." ”				

	A B D 2 a

- **Content validity of the prototype module**

Content validity evaluation is a crucial and intricate step in the tool development process, particularly when measuring complex constructs in social and administrative pharmacy research. This study conducted a content validity evaluation of a developed prototype module to ensure it effectively reflects the intended educational content.

Xu Aiai et al. (2021) suggest that content validity can be assessed using four methods: expert judgment, statistical analysis, retest analysis, and empirical evaluation. Among these, expert judgment is widely used for educational modules. Lynn (1986) emphasized that involving at least five experts can enhance the reliability and representativeness of the results.

In this study, feedback from subject matter experts and experienced educators was used to identify potential issues and make necessary revisions. Five content experts provided ratings and feedback on the module's content.

To systematically evaluate the content validity of the module, the researchers designed an assessment form based on the methods of Almanasreh & Chen (2019), with a simplified example shown in Table 1. Each part of the module was rated by three content experts on a scale from 1 (strongly disagree) to 5 (strongly agree). Additionally, these experts provided valuable comments and suggestions, which helped improve the module's content.

Through this rigorous evaluation process, the researchers ensured the scientific accuracy and reliability of the module content, laying a solid foundation for its application in educational practice.

Table 3.1 Example of the Assessment Form for Content Validity

Lesson number	Specific evaluation indicators	Strongly disagree	Disagree	Neutral	Agree	Strongly agree
	The topic matches the current curriculum	1	2	3	4	5
	Tasks are relevant to the topic	1	2	3	4	5
	Activities match STAD teaching strategies	1	2	3	4	5
1	Evaluation methods objectively reflect student learning outcomes	1	2	3	4	5
	Teaching content stimulates student interest	1	2	3	4	5
	The content is appropriate for the students' cognitive level	1	2	3	4	5
	The topic matches the current curriculum	1	2	3	4	5
	Tasks are relevant to the topic	1	2	3	4	5
	Activities match STAD teaching strategies	1	2	3	4	5
2	Evaluation methods objectively reflect student learning outcomes	1	2	3	4	5
	Teaching content stimulates student interest	1	2	3	4	5
	The content is appropriate for the students' cognitive level	1	2	3	4	5

The content validity level can be calculated using the Percentage Calculation Method (PCM). The formula is as follows::

$$\text{Content Validity Level} = \frac{\text{Total Expert Score}(x)}{\text{Total Maximum Score}(y)} \times 100\%$$

A content validity of 70% or higher indicates high content validity. While traditionally, values lower than 70% were considered unacceptable (Noh & Ahmad, 2005), contemporary research emphasizes the importance of expert consensus and the specific context of the assessment (Lawshe, 1975; Almanasreh et al., 2019)

Table 3.2 Content Validity of the Prototype Module

Items		E1	E2	E3	E4	E5	Total	Mean	Total maximum score	Percentage (PCM)
1	1.1	4	4	4	5	5	22	4.40	25	88.00%
	1.2	5	5	4	4	4	22	4.40	25	88.00%
	1.3	4	5	4	5	5	23	4.60	25	92.00%
	1.4	4	4	5	4	4	21	4.20	25	84.00%
	1.5	4	5	5	5	5	24	4.80	25	96.00%
	1.6	4	5	5	5	4	23	4.60	25	92.00%
2	2.1	4	4	4	4	4	20	4.00	25	80.00%
	2.2	4	4	5	5	4	22	4.40	25	88.00%
	2.3	5	4	4	4	5	22	4.40	25	88.00%

	2.4	4	5	5	5	5	24	4.80	25	96.00%
	2.5	4	5	5	5	5	24	4.80	25	96.00%
	2.6	4	4	4	4	4	20	4.00	25	80.00%
3	3.1	4	5	5	5	5	24	4.80	25	96.00%
	3.2	4	4	4	4	4	20	4.00	25	80.00%
	3.3	4	5	5	5	5	24	4.80	25	96.00%
	3.4	4	5	5	5	5	24	4.80	25	96.00%
	3.5	5	4	5	5	5	24	4.80	25	96.00%
	3.6	4	4	5	3	4	20	4.00	25	80.00%
4	4.1	3	3	5	4	5	20	4.00	25	80.00%
	4.2	4	4	4	4	4	20	4.00	25	80.00%
	4.3	4	4	5	5	4	22	4.40	25	88.00%
	4.4	4	4	4	4	4	20	4.00	25	80.00%
	4.5	3	3	5	4	5	20	4.00	25	80.00%
	4.6	4	4	5	5	4	22	4.40	25	88.00%
5	5.1	4	5	5	5	5	24	4.80	25	96.00%
	5.2	4	5	5	5	5	24	4.80	25	96.00%
	5.3	4	5	5	5	5	24	4.80	25	96.00%
	5.4	4	5	5	5	5	24	4.80	25	96.00%
	5.5	4	4	5	5	4	22	4.40	25	88.00%
	5.6	4	4	4	4	4	20	4.00	25	80.00%
6	6.1	4	4	5	3	4	20	4.00	25	80.00%
	6.2	4	5	5	5	5	24	4.80	25	96.00%
	6.3	4	5	5	5	5	24	4.80	25	96.00%
	6.4	5	4	4	4	5	22	4.40	25	88.00%
	6.5	4	5	5	5	5	24	4.80	25	96.00%
	6.6	4	5	5	5	5	24	4.80	25	96.00%

7	7.1	4	5	5	5	5	24	4.80	25	96.00%
	7.2	4	5	5	5	5	24	4.80	25	96.00%
	7.3	4	4	5	5	4	22	4.40	25	88.00%
	7.4	4	5	5	5	3	22	4.40	25	88.00%
	7.5	4	4	4	4	4	20	4.00	25	80.00%
	7.6	3	4	5	4	4	20	4.00	25	80.00%
8	8.1	3	4	5	4	4	20	4.00	25	80.00%
	8.2	4	4	4	4	4	20	4.00	25	80.00%
	8.3	4	4	3	4	5	20	4.00	25	80.00%
	8.4	4	5	5	5	5	24	4.80	25	96.00%
	8.5	4	4	4	5	5	22	4.40	25	88.00%
	8.6	4	4	4	4	4	20	4.00	25	80.00%
9	9.1	4	5	5	5	4	23	4.60	25	92.00%
	9.2	3	4	5	4	4	20	4.00	25	80.00%
	9.3	4	4	4	4	4	20	4.00	25	80.00%
	9.4	4	5	5	5	4	23	4.60	25	92.00%
	9.5	4	4	4	4	4	20	4.00	25	80.00%
	9.6	4	4	4	4	5	21	4.20	25	84.00%
10	10.1	4	4	4	5	4	21	4.20	25	84.00%
	10.2	4	4	4	4	5	21	4.20	25	84.00%
	10.3	4	4	4	5	4	21	4.20	25	84.00%
	10.4	4	5	5	5	5	24	4.80	25	96.00%
	10.5	4	4	5	4	4	21	4.20	25	84.00%
	10.6	4	4	4	4	4	20	4.00	25	80.00%
11	11.1	4	4	4	4	4	20	4.00	25	80.00%
	11.2	4	5	5	5	5	24	4.80	25	96.00%
	11.3	4	4	4	4	4	20	4.00	25	80.00%

	11.5	4	4	5	5	5	23	4.60	25	92.00%
	11.5	4	5	5	5	5	24	4.80	25	96.00%
	11.6	4	4	4	4	4	20	4.00	25	80.00%
12	12.1	4	4	5	5	4	22	4.40	25	88.00%
	12.2	4	5	5	4	4	22	4.40	25	88.00%
	12.3	4	5	5	5	5	24	4.80	25	96.00%
	12.4	4	4	4	4	4	20	4.00	25	80.00%
	12.5	4	4	5	5	4	22	4.40	25	88.00%
	12.6	4	4	4	4	5	21	4.20	25	84.00%

Table 2 illustrates that each part of the course plan in this module achieved a PCM (Percentage Calculation Method) value of 80.0% or higher, reflecting strong expert validation of the content. Nevertheless, certain sections, specifically 4.1, 4.2, 4.5, 7.6, 8.1, and 9.2, were marked lower by one expert with a score of 3. This prompted the researchers to closely examine the feedback provided and implement necessary revisions to improve these parts of the module.

REFERENCES

Abdelmohsen, M. E., et al. (2020). Quasi-experimental research design. In Methods in Educational Research (pp. 85-110). Springer.

Agwu, U. D., & Nmadu, J. (2023). Students' interactive engagement, academic achievement, and self-concept in chemistry: an evaluation of cooperative learning pedagogy. *Chemistry Education Research and Practice, 24*(2), 688-705.

Akram, W., & Kumar, R. (2017). A study on positive and negative effects of social media on society. *International journal of computer sciences and engineering, 5*(10), 351-354.

Al-Malki, E. A. A., Gulnaz, F., Zahid Javid, C., & Chaudhry, M. Z. (2022). An empirical investigation of the EFL learners attitudes toward the effectiveness of cooperative learning. *SAGE Open, 12*(4), 21582440221141699.10.1177/21582440221141699

Almanasreh, E., Moles, R., & Chen, T. F. (2019). Evaluation of methods used for estimating content validity. *Research in Social and Administrative Pharmacy, 15*(2), 214-221.

Alansari, M., & Rubie-Davies, C. M. (2021). Enablers and barriers to successful implementation of cooperative learning through professional development. *Education sciences, 11*(7), 312.10.3390/educsci11070312

Alwi, A., & Aziz, N. A. (2024). Cooperative learning: Improving students' understanding, social skills, and motivation. *Sosial Humaniora Komunikasi dan Kebijakan Review, 1*(1), 1-5.

Amineh, R. J., & Asl, H. D. (2015). Review of constructivism and social constructivism. *Journal of social sciences, literature and languages, 1*(1), 9-16.

Artino, A. R. (2005). Review of the motivated strategies for learning questionnaire. University of Connecticut.

Aronson, E. (1978). The jigsaw classroom. Sage Publications.

Ausubel, D. P. (1968). *Educational Psychology: A Cognitive View*. Holt, Rinehart and Winston.

Azizi, M., & Rastegar, M. (2020). The effect of cooperative learning on the development of critical thinking skills in EFL learners. *Journal of Language Teaching and Research, 11*(3), 439-446.

Baydas, O., & Genc, M. (2021). The effect of cooperative learning approach on the attitudes of students towards science course. *International Journal of Science and Mathematics Education, 19*(4), 783-797.

Bećirović, S., Dubravac, V., & Brdarević-Čeljo, A. (2022). Cooperative learning as a pathway to strengthening motivation and improving achievement in an EFL classroom. *Sage Open*, *12*(1), 21582440221078016.10.1177/21582440221078016

Behin, B., & Hamidi, S. (2010). Six writers in search of texts: A protocol-based study of L1 and L2 writing. *ELT Journal, 54*(4), 227-267.

Bloom, B. S. (1956). *Taxonomy of Educational Objectives: The Classification of Educational Goals*. Longman.

Boeree, C. G. (2006). Gordon Allport. *Personality theories*, 2-8.

Brau, B., Fox, N., & Robinson, E. (2020). Behaviorism. The Students' Guide to Learning Design and Research.

Bush, J., & Zuidema, L. (2003). Affect in language learning. Cambridge: Cambridge University Press.

Cai Huikun. (2012). Qian Mu's Analects of Confucius-with the academic process and methods as the main axis.

Campbell, C., & Tran, T. L. N. (2023). The 3C Merry-Go-Round: Constructivism, Cognitivism, Connectivism, Etc. In *Technology-Enhanced Learning and the Virtual University* (pp. 203-225). Singapore: Springer Nature Singapore.

Cao Zhongping, Huang Yuesheng, Cheng Kui, & Jiang Li. (2009). Application of social skills scale to Chinese college students. *The Chinese Journal of Clinical Psychology, 17*(1), 34 – 36.

Cavallo, A. M., & Laubach, T. A. (2001). Teaching the tradition: Traditional teaching. *The American Journal of Surgery, 182*(3), 306-309).

Chen, H., Liu, Y., & Zhou, Y. (2018). Cooperative learning in primary school classrooms: A systematic review and meta-analysis. *Educational Research Review, 24*, 183-195.

Chen, J. (2022). Investigation and countermeasures of the current situation of traditional culture practical teaching in higher vocational colleges under the background of "double creation". *Progress: Teaching and Research*, (6), 214-216.

Chen, J., & Liu, J. (2020). An empirical study on the effectiveness of cooperative learning in the teaching of traditional Chinese culture. *Journal of Social Science Education, 19*(2), 43-56.

Chen, L. (2017). The advantages and disadvantages of textbooks. *International Journal of Education and Research, 5*(1), 1-10).

Chen, Q., & Liu, R. (2020). Educational Psychology (3rd Edition). *Higher Education Press.*

Chen, S., Zhang, L., & Zhao, D. (2018). The exploration of cooperative learning mode in the teaching of traditional Chinese culture. *Journal of Wuhu Vocational Institute of Technology, 30*(3), 60-62.

Chen, X. (2016). Traditional Chinese culture in the classroom: A review of research. *Journal of Curriculum and Teaching, 5*(2), 43-49).

Chen, X., & Huang, Q. (2020). The Application of Cooperative Learning in Traditional Chinese Culture Education. *Journal of Higher Education, 41*(7), 57-63.

Chen, Y. (2017). An Analysis of the Characteristics of Chinese Cultural Education in Primary School Curriculum. *Journal of Social Science for Policy Implications, 5*(1), 49-59.

Chen, Y., & Xu, Y. (2019). Research on the Current Situation and Countermeasures of Traditional Chinese Culture Education in Colleges and Universities. In *2019 6th International Conference on Education and Social Science (ICESS 2019).* Atlantis Press.

Chen, Y., & Yu, Q. (2019). Application of Project-Based Learning in Traditional Chinese Culture Education. *Journal of Educational Science Research, 35*(8), 96-101.

Chen,G., 2019. Application of constructivism learning theory in college English teaching. *Overseas English, (18)*, pp.233-234.

Cheng, L., & Wang, Y. (2019). Chinese education: From traditional culture to modernization. *Journal of Education and Learning, 8*(3), 73-78).

Cheng, S. (2019). Dacheng Education: From the Depths of Traditional Culture to the Future. *Chinese Teachers, 05*, 86-91.

Chi, C., & Xu, J. (2018). Current Situation and Analysis of Excellent Traditional Culture Education in Shanghai Private Universities. *Modernization of Education, 5*(12), 102-103.

Chi, J., & Xu, J. (2018). Study on the status quo of traditional culture education in private colleges and universities. *Education Teaching Forum, 07*, 51-52.

Chen, X., & Liu, Y. (2022). Cooperative learning in Chinese primary and secondary education. Education Development Research, 40(6), 89-104.

Cohen, E. G., & Lotan, R. A. (2014). Designing groupwork: Strategies for the heterogeneous classroom. Teachers College Press.

Collins, L. M. (2010). Modern methods for handling missing data. Annual Review of Psychology, 61, 549-576.

Colucci, E., & Lester, D. (2020). A cross-cultural study of attitudes toward suicide among young people in India, Italy and Australia. *International journal of social psychiatry*, *66*(7), 700-706.

Cong, L. (2006). Presumption of guilty in teaching law. *Chinese Teacher, (01).*

Credé, M., & Phillips, L. A. (2011). A meta-analytic review of the motivated strategies for learning questionnaire. Learning and Individual Differences, 21(4), 337–346.

DeRoche, E. F., & Kellogg, S. (2019). The impact of cooperative learning on student motivation and engagement in online courses. *International Journal of Information and Learning Technology, 36*(2), 129-137.

Dewey, J. (1916). Democracy and Education. The Macmillan Company.

Di Barry, & Zhu Ronggui. (2011). Why do we read the Analects of Confucius? *The Open Era, 3*.

Duncan, T. G., & McKeachie, W. J. (2005). The making of the motivated strategies for learning questionnaire. Educational Psychologist, 40(2), 117–128.

Dyson, B., Shen, Y., Xiong, W., & Dang, L. (2022). How cooperative learning is conceptualized and implemented in Chinese physical education: A systematic review of the literature. *ECNU Review of Education, 5*(1), 185-206.

Editorial Department of China Encyclopedia Publishing House. (1985). *China Encyclopedia Publishing House*.

Ede, L., & Lunsford, A. (1990). Singular texts/plural authors: Perspectives on collaborative writing. Southern Illinois University Press.

Erbil, D. G. (2020). A review of flipped classroom and cooperative learning method within the context of Vygotsky theory. *Frontiers in psychology, 11*, 539791.

Erbil, D. G. (2020). Cooperative learning: Theory, principles, and techniques. International Journal of Education and Literacy Studies, 8(2), 108-120.

Erturan Ilker, G., Arslan, Y., & Demirhanc, G. (2014). A validity and reliability study of the motivated strategies for learning questionnaire. Educational Sciences: Theory & Practice, 14(3), 821–833.

Fan, Y. (2021). Confucianism and Its Contemporary Significance. *Journal of Huaqiao University (Philosophy and Social Sciences Edition), 43*(2), 123-128.

Fang, Q. (2011). College students inheriting traditional culture: Status quo, demand and daily life. *Chinese Youth Studies, (7).*

Feigenbaum, K. D. (2024). A Critique of Abraham Maslow and Carl Rogers as Educators. *Journal of Humanistic Psychology, 64*(1), 44-63.

Gage, N. L., & Berliner, D. C. (1998). Educational Psychology (6th ed.). Houghton Mifflin.

Gao, P., & Ru, Z. (2008). On the elements of Chinese traditional culture. *Journal of Anhui Agricultural Sciences, 36*(14), 5901-5902.

Gao, Q., & Liu, R. (2008). Analysis of the Current Situation and Countermeasures of Traditional Culture Education in Colleges and Universities in China. *Innovation, 2008*(05), 120-122.

Gao, X.-H., & Zhao, J.-M. (2022). The concept, principles, methods, and suggestions of cooperative learning. *China University Teaching*, (5).

Gao, Y., & Ru, X. (2008). The significance of traditional Chinese culture education in contemporary universities. *Journal of Beijing University of Aeronautics and Astronautics (Social Sciences Edition), 21*(3), 70-73.

Gergen, K. J. (1992). The social constructionist movement in modern psychology.

Ghaleb, B. D. S. (2024). Effect of Exam-Focused and Teacher-Centered Education Systems on Students' Cognitive and Psychological Competencies. *International Journal of Multidisciplinary Approach Research and Science,* 2(02), 611-631.

Gordon, M. (2020). The Mis-Education of American Teachers. Teachers College Press.

Gresham, F. M., Elliott, S. N., Vance, M. J., & Cook, C. R. (2011). Comparability of the Social Skills Rating System to the Social Skills Improvement System: Content and psychometric comparisons across elementary and secondary age levels. *School Psychology Quarterly*, *26*(1), 27.

Gu, X. (2021, January 27). Educating "real people" in life practice. *China Teachers' Daily, (006)*, 9.

Guo, C. (2016). Research on the penetration of inquiry and cooperative learning in ideological and political teaching. *Asia Pacific Education.*

Gürbüz, R., & Karamete, A. (2020). The effect of cooperative learning on academic achievement in science education: A meta-analysis study. *Journal of Education and Practice, 11*(19), 35-42.

Guzmán, B. M., Montenegro, M. D. S. S., Galán, R. F. J., & Salgado, O. H. (2019). The role of the teacher in cooperative learning: Case High School Adolfo Lopez Mateos of the UAEMEX. *Dilemmas Contemporáneos: Educación, Política y Valores, 6*(2).

Hao, Y. (2017). Confucian teaching in ancient and modern China. *Frontiers of Education in China, 12*(2), 271-283).

Hartman, H. J. (2020). Holistic faculty development: A learner-centered approach. In Developing and supporting multiculturalism and leadership development: International perspectives on humanizing higher education (Vol. 30, pp. 103-125). Emerald Publishing Limited.

Hattie, J. (2009). Visible Learning: A Synthesis of Over 800 Meta-Analyses Relating to Achievement. Routledge.

He, J. (2012). The Application of Cooperative Learning in English Teaching. Journal of Education and Practice, 3(7), 103.

Hu, W. (2007). Cooperative Learning and Construction of the Three-level Network Teaching Mode in the Ideological and Political Course. *Contemporary Education and Culture, 16*(11), 11-12.

Hua, H., Li, Y., Li, C., Li, X., & Li, Y. (2021). Research on the application of multimedia technology in the teaching of traditional Chinese culture. *Education and Modernization, 1*, 78-82).

Huang, H. (2019). Exploring traditional Chinese culture in language teaching. *Journal of Language and Translation, 9*(2), 1-8).

Huang, R., Chen, Y., & Li, J. (2018). An empirical study on the application of cooperative learning methods in Chinese traditional culture education. *Journal of Xi'an University of Architecture and Technology (Social Science Edition), 10*(3), 292-297.

Huang, S., & Huang, S. (2018). Research on the Application of Cooperative Learning Method in Traditional Chinese Culture Teaching. *Chinese Culture and Education, (07)*, 119-121.

Huang, Y., & Zhang, Y. (2019). On the Challenges and Countermeasures of Chinese Traditional Culture Education in Colleges and Universities. *Journal of Guangzhou College of Education, 10*, 80-83.

Hymes, D. (1972). On communicative competence. *Sociolinguistics, 269293*, 269-293.

Ismail, F. A., Bungsu, J., & Shahrill, M. (2023). Improving students' participation and performance in building quantities through think-pair-share cooperative learning. *Indonesian Journal of Educational Research and Technology, 3*(3), 203-216.

Jamaludin, M., & Mokhtar, M. F. (2018). Students team achievement division. *International Journal of Academic Research in Business and Social Sciences, 8*(2), 570-577.

Jiafu, Z. H. E. N. G., & Yaxing, J. I. A. N. G. (2022). The Generation Logic of Chinese Traditional Teachers' Morality. *Journal of Southwest University Social Science Edition*, *48*(2), 223-232.

Jiang, H. (2019). The role of traditional Chinese culture education in promoting college students' moral education. *Journal of Jilin Education Institute, 35*(9), 48-50.

Jeong, Y., Kim, E., Kim, M., & Zhang, J. J. (2019). Exploring relationships among organizational culture, empowerment, and organizational citizenship behavior in the South Korean professional sport industry. *Sustainability*, *11*(19), 5412.

Johnson, D. W. (1994). Cooperative learning in the classroom. Association for Supervision and Curriculum Development, 1250 N. Pitt St., Alexandria, VA 22314.

Johnson, D. W., & Johnson, R. T. (1989). *Cooperation and competition: Theory and research*. Interaction Book Company.

Johnson, D. W., & Johnson, R. T. (1999). Learning together and alone: Cooperative, competitive, and individualistic learning (5th ed.). Allyn and Bacon.

Johnson, D. W., & Johnson, R. T. (2009). An educational psychology success story: Social interdependence theory and cooperative learning. *Educational researcher, 38*(5), 365-379.

Johnson, D. W., & Johnson, R. T. (2014). *Cooperative learning in the classroom.* Edina, MN: Interaction Book Company.

Johnson, D. W., & Johnson, R. T. (2021). Learning together and alone: The history of our involvement in cooperative learning. In *Pioneering perspectives in cooperative learning* (pp. 44-62). Routledge.

Johnson, D. W., & Johnson, R. T. (2017). The impact of cooperative, competitive, and individualistic learning structures on student motivation and achievement. *Middle School, 11 (1)*, 3-12.

Johnson, D. W., Johnson, R. T., & Smith, K. A. (2014). Cooperative learning: Improving university instruction by basing practice on validated theory. *Journal on Excellence in University Teaching, 25*(4), 1-26.

Johnson, R. T., & Johnson, D. W. (2008). Active learning: Cooperation in the classroom. *The annual report of educational psychology in Japan, 47*, 29-30.

Jonassen, D. H. (1991). Objectivism vs. constructivism: Do we need a new philosophical paradigm? *Educational Technology Research and Development, 39*(3), 5-14.

Jones, V., & Jones, L. (2016). Comprehensive Classroom Management: Creating Communities of Support and Solving Problems. Pearson.

Kagan, S. (1981). Writing: The nature, development, and teaching of written communication [Master's thesis, Erlbaum].

Kagan, S. (1992). Cooperative learning. Resources for Teachers.

Khan, N. M., Noreen, M., & Hussaini, M. H. A. (2024). The Impact of Cooperative Learning on Students' Academic Achievement and Social Behavior. *Harf-o-Sukhan, 8(1)*, 339-348.

Khosim, F., & Awang, M. I. (2020). Validity and reliability of the MSLQ Malay version in measuring the level of motivation and self-regulated learning. Int. J. Sci. Technol. Res, 9, 903-905.

Kirschner, P. A., Sweller, J., & Clark, R. E. (2006). Why minimal guidance during instruction does not work: An analysis of the failure of constructivist, discovery, problem-based, experiential, and inquiry-based teaching. *Educational psychologist, 41*(2), 75-86.

Kirschner, P. A., Sweller, J., & Clark, R. E. (2006). Why minimal guidance during instruction does not work: An analysis of the failure of constructivist, discovery, problem-based, experiential, and inquiry-based teaching. *Educational Psychologist, 41*(2), 75-86).

Klang, N., Karlsson, N., Kilborn, W., Eriksson, P., & Karlberg, M. (2021, August). Mathematical problem-solving through cooperative learning—the importance of peer acceptance and friendships. In *Frontiers in Education* (Vol. 6, p. 710296). Frontiers Media SA.10.3389/feduc.2021.710296

Kounin, J. S. (1970). Discipline and Group Management in Classrooms. Holt, Rinehart and Winston.

Lakens, D. (2022). Sample Size Justification. Collabra: Psychology, 8(1), 33267.

Lawshe, C. H. (1975). A quantitative approach to content validity. *Personnel Psychology, 28*(4), 563-575.

Lee, J. C.-K., Zhang, Z., & Yin, H. (2010). Using multidimensional Rasch analysis to validate the Chinese version of the Motivated Strategies for Learning Questionnaire (MSLQ-CV). European Journal of Psychology of Education, 25(1), 141–155.

Lenkauskaitė, J., Colomer, J., & Bubnys, R. (2020). Students' social construction of knowledge through cooperative learning. *Sustainability, 12*(22), 9606.

Lewin, K. (1947). Frontiers in Group Dynamics: Concept, Method and Reality in Social Science; Social Equilibria and Social Change. Human Relations, 1(1), 5-41.

Linn, R. L., Baker, E. L., & Dunbar, S. B. (2018). Performance-based Assessment: Implications for Large-scale Testing. Educational Researcher.

Li, H., Li, Y., & Liu, C. (2020). The effect of cooperative learning on primary school students' learning outcomes. *Journal of Educational Studies, 11*, 90-97.

Li, J. (2016). An analysis of the status quo and countermeasures of traditional culture education in colleges and universities. *Journal of Fujian Agriculture and Forestry University (Philosophy and Social Sciences), 15*(4), 114-118.

Li, J. (2016). The current situation and challenges of traditional culture education in colleges and universities. *Journal of Changzhou Vocational College of Information Technology, 13*(3), 94-96.

Li, J. (2019). Analysis of the application of cooperative learning method in traditional Chinese culture education. *Journal of Baicheng Normal University, 38*(4), 95-98.

Li, L., & Zhang, S. (2018). Enhancing college students' traditional culture literacy through cooperative learning: A case study of the course of Chinese traditional culture. *Journal of Curriculum and Teaching, 7*(1), 60-68.

Li, M.,2019. Research on strategies to improve social skills of college students based on Situational Learning Theory. *Journal of Higher Education, 40(07)*, pp.139-143.

Li, X. (2017). Analysis of the teaching model of traditional culture in universities. *Journal of Jilin Institute of Chemical Technology, 34*(1), 83-85.

Li, X., & Ma, Y. (2018). Application of Experiential Learning in Traditional Chinese Culture Education. *Journal of Educational Science Research, 34*(3), 69-72.

Li, X., & Ma, Y. (2018). Reflections on the Practice of Traditional Chinese Culture Education in Colleges and Universities. *Journal of Liaoning Normal University (Social Science Edition), 4*, 66-70.

Li, X.D. & Chen, Q., 2020. The enlightenment of sociocultural theory on college English teaching reform under modern educational technology environment. *Digital Communication World, (04)*, pp.274+276.

Li, Y. (2017). Teaching and learning in Confucianism. Journal of South-Central University for Nationalities (Humanities and Social Sciences), 37(4), 110-114.

Li, Y., & Li, N. (2021). Using Tao to control techniques: Persistence and transcendence of teaching methods. *Curriculum, Teaching Materials, Teaching Methods, 41*(6), 45-51.

Li, Z. (2017). On the evaluation standard of Chinese excellent traditional culture. *Social Science Front, (8)*, 1-9.

Liang, S., & 梁漱溟. (1921). Eastern and Western Cultures and Their Philosophies (东西文化及其哲学). *Complete Works of LIANG Shuming, 1989-1993*.

Lu Cuiwei & Zhang Bai Xun. (2022). The traditional cultural implication of Xi Jinping thought on a community with a shared future for mankind. Journal of Mudanjiang Normal University (Social Science Edition) (05),49-58.doi:10.13815/j.cnki.jmtc (pss). 2022.05.002.

Lin, C. (2003). *Dictionary of Psychology*. Shanghai Education Press.

Liu, J. (2013). Confucianism and the Education of the Chinese People. *Education Journal, 2*(4), 147-152).

Liu, J., Wang, Q., & Li, X. (2023). Traditional vs. Cooperative Learning: A Comparative Study. Journal of Educational Research, 45(2), 123-137.

Liu, M., Zhang, S., Cui, J., & Yang, W. (2023). Experimental study of the cooperative learning teaching model in college physical education teaching - Taking the geological physical education course of China University of Geosciences (Beijing) as an example. *China Geological Education, 32*(3), 120-124.

Liu, X. (2019). Challenges to Traditional Chinese Culture Teaching in Modern Chinese Society. *Higher Education Forum, (3)*, 69-71.

Liu, X., Wang, Y., & Wu, Y. (2020). The impact of cooperative learning on students' social-emotional learning outcomes. *Journal of Research in Education for Sustainability, 12*(2), 372-385.

Liu, Y. (2019). Research on the application of cooperative learning method in the teaching of traditional Chinese culture in primary schools. *Journal of Pioneering Education, (11)*, 47-49.

Liu, Y., & Wang, Y. (2019). A Study on the Current Situation and Development of Chinese Traditional Culture Education in Primary and Secondary Schools in China. In *2019 International Conference on Information Technology and Education Technology (ITET 2019).* Atlantis Press.

Liu, Y., Li, X., & Chen, X. (2019). The effect of digital textbook on students' motivation in traditional Chinese culture teaching. *International Journal of Emerging Technologies in Learning, 14*(12), 78-86).

Li, Y., Zhang, Y. A., & Shi, W. (2020). Navigating geographic and cultural distances in international expansion: The paradoxical roles of firm size, age, and ownership. *Strategic Management Journal, 41*(5), 921-949.

Lu, A. (2019). Effective development of "group cooperative learning" in political teaching from the perspective of game theory. *Education Modernization Professional Committee of Guangdong Education Society*, 74-76.

Luo, D. (2014). The Socialist Core Values Education of Contemporary College Students from the Perspective of Cultural Identity. *Ideological Education Research, 2014*(02).

Luo, J., & Liu, J. (2019). Analysis of the Current Situation of Traditional Culture Education in Chinese Universities. *Chinese and Foreign Entrepreneurs, 2019*(09), 194.

Luo, X., & Liu, J. (2019). An Empirical Study on the Traditional Cultural Education of College Students in China. *International Journal of Emerging Technologies in Learning, 14*(16), 88-100. doi: 10.3991/ijet.v14i16.10168

Luo, Y., & Liu Jian. (2019). Investigation on the knowledge and understanding of traditional Chinese culture among college students. *Journal of Henan Institute of Science and Technology (Social Science Edition), 20*(2), 67-70.

Luo, Z. (2002). *Consumer Psychology* (Second Edition). Tsinghua University Press.

Lyman, F. (1981). The responsive classroom discussion: The inclusion of all students. Mainstreaming Digest, 109-113.

Lynn, M. R. (1986). Determination and quantification of content validity. *Nursing Research, 35*(6), 382-386.

Ma, J., Yu, S., & Liu, J. (2018). Discussion on the cultivation of college students' awareness of traditional Chinese culture. *Journal of Guizhou University for Ethnic Minorities, 39*(1), 22-26.

Ma, X.D., Liu, Q. & Meng, X.C.,2019. A review of research on situational learning theory. *Contemporary Educational Theory and Practice, 5(18)*, pp.13-16+30.

Ma, Y., Jiang, Y., & Li, Y. (2018). The current status and problems of traditional culture education in colleges and universities. *Journal of Hebei Normal University (Educational Science Edition), 1*, 76-81.

Maun, D., Shukla, K. D., & Chand, V. S. (2020). Validating motivated strategies for learning questionnaire and invariance test across gender and caste groups in India. Cogent Education, 7(1), 1853303.

Marx, K., & Engels, F. (1972). *The Complete Works of Marx and Engels* (Volume 23). People's Publishing House.

Marsden, E., & Torgerson, C. J. (2012). Single group, pre- and post-test research designs: Some methodological concerns. Oxford Review of Education, 38(5), 583-616.

Maslow, A. H. (1943). Preface to motivation theory. *Psychosomatic medicine*, *5*(1), 85-92.

Men, L. R., & Robinson, K. L. (2018). It's about how employees feel! examining the impact of emotional culture on employee–organization relationships. *Corporate Communications: An International Journal, 23*(4), 470-491.

Maxwell, J. A. (2016). Expanding the history and range of mixed methods research. Journal of Mixed Methods Research, 10(1), 12-2

McGregor, J. L. (1961). Modern Probability Theory and Its Applications (Emanuel Parzen). *SIAM Review, 3*(2), 184.

Mendo-Lázaro, S., León-del-Barco, B., Polo-del-Río, M. I., & López-Ramos, V. M. (2022). The impact of cooperative learning on university students' academic goals. *Frontiers in Psychology, 12*, 787210. 10.3389/fpsyg.2021.787210

Merriam, S. B., & Bierema, L. L. (2013). Adult Learning: Linking Theory and Practice. Jossey-Bass.

Miguel, J. M., de Blas, C. S., Rodríguez, F. A., & Sipols, A. G. (2023). Collaborative learning in management subjects to university students: A multi-level research to identify group profile, engagement and academic performance. *The International Journal of Management Education, 21*(1), 100762.

Millis, B. (Ed.). (2023). Cooperative learning in higher education: Across the disciplines, across the academy. Taylor & Francis.

Millis, B. J. (2023). Cooperative learning: It's not just group work. Techniques for College and University Teaching.

Mohamed Abobaker, R., Sulaiman Alamri, M., Alshaery, B., & M Hamdan-Mansour, A. (2023). Impact of Jigsaw Cooperative Learning Strategy on academic achievement and opinion among Nursing Students. *Journal of Holistic Nursing And Midwifery, 33*(1), 43-51.10.32598/jhnm.33.1.2344

Moore, K. S., & Corter, J. E. (2022). The effectiveness of cooperative activities in promoting individual learning. *Teaching Learning for Effective Instruction, 223*.

Mulyana, F., Juniar, D. T., Malik, A. A., Mulyana, D., & Hanief, Y. N. (2024). The Influence of Cooperative Learning Models and Learning Styles on Social Skills in University Student.

Neri, M. T., & Miri, B. (2020). Cooperative learning and creativity in science education: A systematic review. *Thinking Skills and Creativity, 38*, 100722.

Nisar, N., & Hussain, M. S. (2023). Learner vs Teacher Centered Classes: Critical Discourse Analysis of Stakeholders' Stance from Socio-Cognitive Perspective. *Global Social Sciences Review, VIII*, 191-200.

Niu, Y., Li, J., Zhang, Q., & Huang, Y. (2018). Research on the application of cooperative learning in the teaching of Chinese culture and history in colleges and universities. *Higher Education Forum, 11*, 57-61.

Patton, M. Q. (2015). Qualitative research and evaluation methods (4th ed.). Thousand Oaks, CA: Sage.

Pan, Y.C. & Wu, H.J.,2018. The application of active learning in higher education. *Research in Educational Development, 38(08)*, pp.105-110.

Panitz, T. (2010). Collaborative versus cooperative learning: A comparison of the two concepts which will help us understand the underlying nature of interactive learning.

Peng, N. (2011). On the Strategies of Cooperative Learning in Phonetics Teaching for English Majors. *Journal of Educational Science of Hunan Normal University*, 118-120.

Piaget, J. (1926). Children's Concepts of the World.

Piaget, J. (1967). On the development of memory and identity.

Pintrich, P. R., & Schunk, D. H. (2002). Motivation in education: Theory, research, and applications. Pearson.

Pintrich, P. R., Smith, D. A. F., Garcia, T., & McKeachie, W. J. (1991). *A Manual for the Use of the Motivated Strategies for Learning Questionnaire (MSLQ).* National Center for Research to Improve Postsecondary Teaching and Learning.

Pritchett, L. (2015). Creating education systems coherent for learning outcomes: Making the transition from schooling to learning. *Research on Improving Systems of Education (RISE).*

Qi, J. (2010). Looking at the lack of traditional culture of contemporary college students from the differences between Chinese and Western cultures. *Heilongjiang Higher Education Research, (3).*

Qian, M. (1996). Outline of National History.

Ornstein, A. C., & Hunkins, F. P. (2017). Curriculum: Foundations, Principles, and Issues. Pearson.

Radjabova, S. (2023). Group cooperative learning and its effectiveness. Journal of Educational Research and Practice, 13(1), 45-59.

Radjabova, I. R. (2023). Organization of the Educational Process on the Basis of Cooperative Pedagogy Theoretical And Methodological Foundations of Education. *Journal of Pedagogical Inventions and Practices, 27*, 25-28..

Rao Zongyi, & Li Wenru. (2008). Rao Zongyi: Academic and art. *The Forbidden City, (9)*, 17-34.

Rao, N. (1995). Motivational beliefs, study strategies and exam performance in Chinese high and low achievers. In Society for Research in Child Development Conference.

Rao, N., Moely, B. E., & Sachs, J. (2000). Motivational beliefs, study strategies, and mathematics attainment in high- and low-achieving chinese secondary school students. Contemporary Educational Psychology, 25(3), 287–316.

Rao, Y. (2014). Research on the Role of Traditional Chinese Culture in the Ideological and Political Education of College Students. *Journal of Guangdong University of Education, 35*(3), 99-104.

Ridwan, M. R., & Hadi, S. (2022). A meta-analysis study on the effectiveness of a cooperative learning model on vocational high school students' mathematics learning outcomes. *Participatory Educational Research*, *9*(4), 396-421.10.17275/per.22.97.9.4

Riggio, R. E. (2014). The Social Skills Inventory (SSI): measuring nonverbal and social skills. The sourcebook of nonverbal measures, 25-33.

Risma Margaretha, S., Albet Maydiantoro, A., Onojah Amos, O., Dwi Yulianti, Y., Suparman, A., Basri, M., ... & Suroto, S. (2022). Reasoning model and moral simulation to improve students' social skills: A focused look at emotional intelligence. *Journal of Educational and Social Research*, *12*(1), 335-345.10.36941/jesr-2022-0026

Roger, T., & Johnson, D. W. (1994). An overview of cooperative learning. *Creativity and collaborative learning, 14*(2), 1-21.

Rogers, C. R. (1951). Perceptual reorganization in client-centered therapy.

Salamah, E. R., Rifayanti, Z. E. T., & Trisnawaty, W. (2024). The effect of cooperative learning model on elementary school students' learning motivation. *Scientific Journal of Basic Education, 11*(1), 18-31.

Salamah, E. R., Rifayanti, Z. E. T., & Trisnawaty, W. (2024). The effect of cooperative learning model on elementary school students' learning motivation. *Jurnal Ilmiah Pendidikan Dasar, 11(1)*, 18-31.

Salih, M. M. M., Hashim, R. S., & Kasim, M. A. (2021). Forecasting Achievement Sports through Cooperative Learning in Handball Training in Physical Education. *Annals of Applied Sport Science*, *9*(3), 0-0.10.52547/aassjournal.953

Salimi, M., & Dardiri, A. (2021). The Profile of Students' Social Skills of Bengawan Solo Elementary Nature School. *European Journal of Educational Research, 10*(1), 211-226. 10.12973/eu-jer.10.1.211

Savery, J. R., & Duffy, T. M. (1996). Problem-based learning: An instructional model and its constructivist framework. *Educational Technology, 36*(1), 31-38.

Shafi, S., & Masood, M. H. (2023). Pedagogical Approaches in English Language Learning (ELL): Comparative Analysis of Teacher-centred Approach and Student-centred Approach. *Research Highlights in Language, Literature and Education*, 68-77.

Sharon, S. (1976). Cooperative learning in small groups. Review of Educational Research, 46(4), 123-144.

Sharan, S., & Sharan, Y. (1992). Expanding cooperative learning through group investigation. Teachers College Press.

Shen, H., & Comrey, A. L. (1997). Predicting medical students' academic performances by their cognitive abilities and personality characteristics. *Academic Medicine*, *72*(9), 781-6.

Shi, J. (2021). Revisiting the application of teaching method. *Occupation, 16*, 46-48.

Shinde, S. M., & Shinde, M. B. (2022). EFFECTIVENESS OF COOPERATIVE LEARNING TECHNIQUES IN TEACHING COMMUNICATION SKILLS: ESP LEARNERS'PERSPECTIVE. *Journal of Teaching English for Specific and Academic Purposes*, 001-012. 10.22190/jtesap2201001s

Shirley, D., & Irani, T. (2020). Traditional teaching methods. In *Encyclopedia of Education Economics and Finance* (pp. 1-8). Springer.

Sibomana, A., Karegeya, C., & Sentongo, J. (2021). Effect of Cooperative Learning on Chemistry Students' Achievement in Rwandan Day-Upper Secondary Schools. *European Journal of Educational Research*, *10*(4), 2079-2088.10.12973/eu-jer.10.4.2079

Silva, R., Farias, C., & Mesquita, I. (2021). Cooperative learning contribution to student social learning and active role in the class. *Sustainability, 13*(15), 8644.10.3390/su13158644

Slavin, R. E. (1983). Cooperative Learning. *Research on Teaching Monograph Series.* Longman Inc., College Division, 1560 Broadway, New York, NY 10036.

Slavin, R. E. (2013). Cooperative learning and achievement: Theory and research.

Slavin, R. E. (2014). Cooperative learning and academic achievement: Why does groupwork work? *Anales de Psicología, 30*(3), 785-791.

Slavin, R. E. (2015). Cooperative learning and academic achievement: Why does groupwork work? *Anales de Psicología, 31*(2), 552-558.

Slavin, R.E., 2019. Cooperative learning: Contemporary research on cooperative learning in elementary English classes. *British Journal of Educational Psychology, 1(1-2)*, pp.258-264.

Song, Z., Cao, Y., & Liu, Y. (2020). The effect of cooperative learning on students' motivation and engagement in physical education. *Journal of Beijing Sport University, 43*(5), 71-79.

State Council of the People's Republic of China. (2016). Reply of the State Council on the Overall Planning of Jinan City. Retrieved from https://www.gov.cn/

Stoddard, A. W., & Grosskopf, K. (2018). Cooperative learning in higher education: A review of research. *Journal of Cooperative Education and Internships, 51*(1), 9-27).

Su, Y. (2022). The Importance of Traditional Chinese Culture in Contemporary College Students' Value Education. *China Journal of Ideology and Theory, 15*(1), 29-33.

Sulistyowati, S., & Jubaidah, S. (2024). Improving social skills and learning outcomes with carousel feedback and inside outside circle modification methods. *Research Journal on Teacher Professional Development, 2*(1), 1-13.

Sun, J., & Wang, L. (2004). Task design of cooperative learning in English class. Journal of Chengdu Electromechanical College, 3, 75-77.

Tabachnick, B. G., Fidell, L. S., & Ullman, J. B. (2013). *Using multivariate statistics* (Vol. 6, pp. 497-516). Boston, MA: Pearson.

Tamimy, M., Rashidi, N., & Koh, J. H. L. (2023). The use of cooperative learning in English as a foreign language classes: The prevalence, fidelity, and challenges. *Teaching and Teacher Education, 121*, 103915.

Tang, Y. (2018). Teaching Traditional Chinese Culture: A Case Study of "Literature and Culture of the Tang Dynasty." *Journal of Language and Education Research, 3*(3), 81-88).

Taylor, R. T. (2012). Review of the Motivated Strategy for Learning Questionnaire (MSLQ) using reliability generalization techniques to assess scale reliability (Ph.D. dissertation). Auburn University.

Thelen, H. (1954). Dynamics of groups at work. University of Chicago Press.

Topping, K. (1996). The effectiveness of peer tutoring in further and higher education: A typology and review of the literature. Higher Education, 32(3), 321-345.

Tuckman, J. A. C. O. B. (1935). A picture performance scale. *Journal of Educational Psychology*, *26*(1), 17.

Tuckman, B. W. (1965). Developmental sequence in small groups. Psychological Bulletin, 63, 384-399.

Turgunova, F., & Abdurahimovna, R. S. (2023). Interactive teaching methods in English classes. *Journal of Foreign Languages and Linguistics, 5*(5).

Vygotsky, L. (1986). Thought and Language, trans. and ed. In Kozulin. Kozulin, A. (1986). The concept of activity in Soviet psychology: Vygotsky, his disciples and critics. *American psychologist, 41*(3), 264.

Vygotsky, L. S. (1978). Mind in society: The development of higher psychological processes. Harvard University Press.

Vygotsky, L. S. (2018). *Lecture Notes on Psychology*. Jilin Publishing Group.

Vygotsky, L. S., & Cole, M. (1978). *Mind in society: Development of higher psychological processes*. Harvard university press.

Wachyunni, S. (2015). Scaffolding and co-operative learning: Effects on reading comprehension and vocabulary knowledge in English as a foreign language.

Waite-Stupiansky, S. (2022). Jean Piaget's constructivist theory of learning. In *Theories of early childhood education* (pp. 3-18). Routledge.

Wang, C. (2023). Resurgence of Confucian education in contemporary China: Parental involvement, moral anxiety, and the pedagogy of memorisation. *Journal of Moral Education, 52*(3), 325-342.

Wang, H. W. (2023). The impact of integrating social media into cooperative learning on students' knowledge sharing behavior: A perspective from equity theory and foundational interpersonal relationship theory. *Journal of Digital Learning and Technology, 15*(2), 85-121.

Wang, H., & Zhang, S. (2021). The Application of Cooperative Learning in Traditional Chinese Culture Education: An Empirical Study. *Modern Educational Technology, 31*(4), 106-111.

Wang, H., Sun, X., & Chen, H. (2013). Application of cooperative learning in university classroom. *Academic Exchange, 1*, 215-216.

Wang, H., Wang, S., & Sun, Y. (2021). The effectiveness of cooperative learning on students' academic achievement. *Journal of Research in Education for Ethnic Minorities, 5*(1), 76-82).

Wang, J. (2016). Exploration and reflection on traditional Chinese culture education in universities. *China University Teaching, (8)*, 69-71.

Wang, L. (2019). Exploration and Practice of Integrating Excellent Traditional Chinese Culture into Classroom Teaching Materials in Vocational Education: Taking the Outline of Excellent Traditional Chinese Culture as an Example. *Guangdong Vocational and Technical Education and Research, (6)*, 4.

Wang, L., & Liu, L. (2020). The Challenges and Countermeasures of Traditional Chinese Culture Education in Colleges and Universities. *Journal of Guangzhou University (Social Science Edition), 19*(4), 102-108.

Wang, X. (2021). Traditional Chinese Culture. In Y. Fang, L. Sun, & Z. Zhang (Eds.), *The Palgrave Handbook of Chinese Culture and Society* (pp. 1-14). Palgrave Macmillan.

Wang, X. Y., Wang, R. F., Luo, Y., Qiao, X. M., & Qi, H. M. (2021). A study on the reasons for the lack of awareness of traditional Chinese culture among university students and countermeasures—A case study of universities in Inner Mongolia. *Talents, (2)*, 62-64.

Wang, X., & Li, H. (2018). On the application of performance-based evaluation method in Chinese teaching. *Journal of Higher Education Research, (5), 78-81).

Wang, X.J.,2020. Exploration of motivation strategies in college English teaching based on Self-determination Theory. *Language and Culture Communication, 6(04)*, pp.86-89.

Wang, Y. (2016). On the inheritance and development of excellent traditional Chinese culture education in colleges and universities. *Education Teaching Forum, (21)*, 110-111.

Webb, N. M., & Palincsar, A. S. (1996). Group processes in the classroom. In D. C. Berliner & R. C. Calfee (Eds.), *Handbook of educational psychology* (pp. 841-873). Macmillan.

Wenhua, C. (2006). Traditional Confucianism in modern China: Ma Yifu's ethical thought. *Frontiers of Philosophy in China, 1*(3), 366-381.

Wu, H. (2021). Common Sense of Chinese History. *Emergency Management Press.*

Wu, R., & He, G. (2014). Research on the application effect of cooperative learning in college English writing teaching. *Foreign Language Teaching, 35*(3), 44-47.

Wu, X., & Yang, J. (2020). The traditional teaching method in the Chinese culture context. *Journal of Language Teaching and Research, 11*(4), 1557-1564).

Xi, J. (2015). His speech at the Symposium on Literature and Art [Newspaper article]. *People's Daily.*

Xie, H., & Wu, X. (2019). The effect of cooperative learning on students' English writing skills. *Journal of Foreign Languages and Their Teaching, 11*, 42-49.

Xie, J., Li, L., & Jiang, Y. (2018). Rote learning and its cultural factors in Chinese education. *Frontiers of Education in China, 13*(2), 173-182).

Xie, T., Zhou, J., Liu, J. H., & Liao, C. C. (2021). How does a historical system of meaning weigh on the present? Social representations of Confucianism and their role in young Chinese lives in the People's Republic of China. *Psychology and Developing Societies, 33*(1), 73-102.

Xie, X. (2019). Problems and Countermeasures of Chinese Traditional Culture Education in Colleges and Universities. *Journal of Xinjiang University (Philosophy, Humanities and Social Sciences), 5*, 94-98.

Xu, X., & Li, X. (2018). The Significance of Calligraphy in Chinese Culture and Its Role in Chinese Teaching. *Journal of Higher Education and Vocational Education, 8*(4), 127-129).

Xu, A., Chen, C., Xiang, Y., Zou, R., & Hong, X. (2021). Content validity: An indispensable validity indicator in the development of sports psychology scales. *Advances in Psychology, 11*, 1981.

Xue, J. X. (2023). The connotation and practice of the educational value of the Analects under the "from the extensive to the intensive" educational philosophy. *Theory and Practice of Education, 43*(33), 41-45.

Yassin, A. A., Razak, N. A., & Maasum, N. R. M. (2018). Cooperative learning: General and theoretical background. Advances in Social Sciences Research Journal, 5(8), 642-654.

Yan, S. (2020). Current situation and challenges of Chinese traditional culture education. *Journal of International Education Development, 40*(2), 13-23.

Yan, X. (2020). Chinese traditional culture education in colleges and universities: Current status and challenges. *Journal of International Education Development, 42*(1), 50-58.

Yang Chaoming (2016). *The Wisdom of the Analects of Confucius*. London: Routledge.

Yang, D. (2024). A discussion on high school Chinese language learning methods. *Modern Education and Practice, 3*(8).

Yang, W., & Ye, Y. (2020). Research on the application of cooperative learning method in the teaching of Chinese traditional culture. *Journal of Primary and Secondary School Curriculum, (11)*, 51-54.

Yazici, H. J., 2016. A comparison of cooperative learning and traditional learning activities in computer programming courses. *Interactive Learning Environments, 24(1)*, 37-51.

Ye Jiaying (1996). *The Interpretation of the Analects of Confucius*. Beijing: China Social Sciences Press.

Ye, H. (2014). *History and System of Western Psychology* (2nd Edition). People's Education Press.

Ye, H. (2014). Study on the social interdependence of students in classroom teaching. *Journal of Xiangnan University, 16*(3), 105-108.

Yeh, H., & Inman, A. (2007). Cultural foundations of education: Traditional Chinese thought. Pearson.

Yeh, Q. (2023). Challenges and difficulties of cooperative learning. *Taiwanese Journal of Education Review, 12*(6), 114-118.

Yeni, Z. F. (2024). Efforts to improve learning outcomes with the Cooperative Learning type Student Teams Achievement Division in Class VII of SMP Negeri 6 Rokan IV Koto. *Journal of Community Service and Educational Research, 2*(3), 270-276.

Yu, A. C. (2019). Chinese culture and globalization. In L. Chen & H. Li (Eds.), *China's global rebalancing and the new Silk Road* (pp. 85-104). Palgrave Macmillan.

Yu, J. Y. (2023). Current status analysis and strategy research on the integration of excellent traditional Chinese culture into the "Advanced German" course. *Creative Education Studies, 11*, 895.

Yu, Y., & Wang, Q. (2019). Research on the application of cooperative learning method in the teaching of traditional Chinese culture. *Journal of Xiamen University, 56*(6), 127-131.

Zamani, M., & Huang, X. H. (2016). *Mind in society: The development of higher psychological processes* [Master's thesis, Harvard University Press].

Zhang, H. (2016). The use of storytelling in the classroom: A reflection on traditional Chinese culture. *Journal of Language and Literature Education, 4*(2), 45-52).

Zhang, H. (2019). Research on Cultivating Cultural Confidence with Chinese Excellent Traditional Culture.

Zhang, H. (2020). The value and significance of traditional Chinese culture education in colleges and universities. *Journal of Inner Mongolia Normal University (Philosophy and Social Sciences Edition), 49*(5), 131-133.

Zhang, H., & Liu, J. (2018). Reflections on the Development of Chinese Traditional Culture Education in Higher Vocational Colleges. *Journal of Jilin Vocational and Technical College of Communications, 4*, 68-71.

Zhang, J. (2019). The Dilemma and Coping Strategies of Youth Traditional Culture Education. *Moral Education, 07*, 31.

Zhang, J., Han, L., Chen, H., & Liu, Z. (2020). Application of cooperative learning in physical education of universities. *Journal of Guangdong University of Technology (Social Sciences Edition), 19*(4), 13-18.

Zhang, M., & Li, J. (2020). Application of Gamification in Traditional Chinese Culture Education. *Journal of Inner Mongolia Agricultural University (Social Science Edition), 4*, 62-66.

Zhang, M., & Li, J. (2020). Reflections on the Teaching of Traditional Chinese Culture in Colleges and Universities. *Journal of Inner Mongolia Agricultural University (Social Science Edition), 4*, 62-66.

Zhang, M., & Li, J. (2021). The Application of Cooperative Learning in Traditional Chinese Culture Education. *Journal of Chongqing Technology and Business University (Social Science Edition), 38*(1), 50-57.

Zhang, P. G., & Bao, J. (2024). Survey study on the current situation of traditional Chinese cultural education among contemporary college students—A case study of a local polytechnic university. *Modern Education and Practice, 3*(2).

Zhang, Q., & Wang, Y. (2019). Review of research on Chinese traditional culture education. *Journal of Guangdong University of Education, 39*(1), 33-38).

Zhang, W. (2019). Analysis of political teaching from the perspective of cooperative learning. *Gansu Education, 11*, 64.

Zhang, Y. (2024). Research on the Current Situation and Countermeasures of Excellent Traditional Chinese Culture Education among College Students: A Case Study of Universities in Qingdao. (Doctoral dissertation, Qingdao University of Science and Technology).

Zhang, Y., & Huang, Y. (2018). The Current Situation and Problems of Traditional Chinese Culture Education in Colleges and Universities. *Journal of Changchun University of Science and Technology (Social Sciences Edition), 1*, 59-61.

Zhao, S. (2018). Research on the transformation of evaluation methods in the teaching of traditional Chinese culture. *Chinese and Foreign Education, (9), 129-131).

Zhao, X. (2008). A New Path to Moral Education. *Marxism and Reality, 2008*(06), 176-178.

Zhou, H., & Zhu, Y. (2018). Reflections on the Teaching of Chinese Traditional Culture in Colleges and Universities. *Journal of Jiamusi Vocational Institute, 12*, 55-58.

Zhou, T., Li, X., & Wei, Y. (2014). Investigation and reflection on the current situation of contemporary college students' cognition of traditional culture. *China Electric Power Education, 20*, 89-90+108.

Zhou, Y., Li, X., & Wang, F. (2014). Reflections on the traditional culture education in the era of the Internet. *Journal of North China University of Water Resources and Electric Power (Social Science Edition), 26*(1), 48-50.

Zonggui, L. (2015). Between tradition and modernity: Philosophical reflections on the modernization of Chinese culture. Chartridge Books Oxford.